GW01080977

Sarah's Letters

Bedford Way Papers   ISSN 0261—0078

Sarah's Letters
A Case of Shyness

Bernard T Harrison
Edited and with an introduction by Fred Murphy

Bedford Way Papers 26
Institute of Education, University of London
distributed by Turnaround Distribution Ltd.

First published in 1986 by the Institute of Education, University of London,
20 Bedford Way, London WC1H 0AL.

Distributed by Turnaround Distribution Ltd., 27 Horsell Road,
London N5 1XL (telephone: 01-609 7836).

Cover design by Herb Gillman

The opinions expressed in these papers are those of the authors and do not necessarily reflect those of the publisher.

© Institute of Education, University of London, 1986
All rights reserved.

ISBN   0   85473   241   1

British Library Cataloguing in Publication Data

Harrison, Bernard T.
  Sarah's letters: a case of shyness — (Bedford Way papers, ISSN 0261-0078; 26)
  1. School children — Psychology   2. Bashfulness in children
  I. Title   II. Murphy, Fred   III. Series 370.15   LB1139.E5

  ISBN 0-85473-241-1

Printed in Great Britain by Reprographic Services
Institute of Education, University of London.
Typesetting by Joan Rose

126-001-081-1285

Contents

Note on Author

Bernard T. Harrison is Senior Lecturer in Education at the University of Sheffield. His writings include *Learning through Writing: stages of growth in English* (Windsor: NFER-Nelson, 1983) and, as editor, *English Studies, 11-18: an arts-based approach* (London: Hodder and Stoughton, 1983). Dr Harrison is a past Postgraduate Certificate in Education student of the University of London Institute of Education.

Fred Murphy, editor, is Lecturer in the Department of English and Media Studies, University of London Institute of Education.

Acknowledgements

Thanks are due to the following: Lawrence Pollinger Ltd and the Estate of Mrs Frieda Lawrence Ravagli for permission to quote the poem 'Conscience' by D.H. Lawrence; Scottish Academic Press (Journals) Ltd for permission to quote a poem which appeared in *Use of English;* and George Allen and Unwin for permission to quote Arthur Waley's translation of the poem of Po Chü-i, 'Being visited by a friend during illness'.

Editor's Introduction
Fred Murphy

We human beings seem very prone to divide our experiences into two categories. For example, Henry James imagines young Basil Ransom in *The Bostonians* considering that 'the simplest division it is possible to make of the human race is into the people who take things hard and the people who take them easy'. A similar crude analysis would be offered by many teachers to a newcomer taking over their class: there are the pupils who make trouble, and those who are no trouble. If we accept for the moment both these classifications, we are here offered a rare opportunity to enter the world of a schoolgirl who takes things hard, but is no trouble. The misery endured by quiet, withdrawn pupils is easily overlooked; Sarah's letters illustrate the pain which is inflicted on them by the more or less placid, tedious and mediocre routine which, rather than violence or serious disorder, is still normal in our secondary schools, places where for many young people 'the grayness of our daily lives has an abrasive potency of its own'.[1] Overlooked by teachers, these pupils may also be rejected by their peers; recent evidence in another Bedford Way Paper[2] suggests that girls are likely to see shyness as a negative characteristic, engendering dislike rather than sympathy.

The letters communicate a deepening dissidence from her schools — a rebellion of a kind likely to be expressed in silence, absence, early leaving, or disappointing examination results, rather than aggression. Her unhappiness takes her to the border of 'that minimal confidence in the world which is called sanity'[3] but even when her pain seems greatest her exceptional capacity for analysis is directed outwards onto her school, the teachers and other pupils, as well as inwards. Thus the letters she wrote to Dr Harrison may speak valuably to others who work in schools or have contact with the young. Together with his discussion of a teacher's possible therapeutic role, the letters should be of special concern to students and teachers in the sphere of teacher education. Students focus strongly on learning to manage their classes and to teach their own subject. Noisy, active troublemakers preoccupy them. People like Sarah may be entirely overlooked. Only if courses involve students in prolonged encounters with individual pupils may the students realize the intense need many pupils have for an attentive listener who can communicate a sense of the pupil's value. Often it is never having received this quality of attention which is at the root of learning difficulties. And as Simone Weil said, 'those who are unhappy have no need for anything in this world but people capable of giving them their attention'. [4]

Any sympathetic, accessible teacher may receive such confidences as Sarah entrusted to Dr Harrison: those who run sports teams or school journeys, those who teach art or craft subjects which encourage a less formal environment, those who do not make themselves scarce as soon as the lesson ends. English teachers are likely recipients, since they probably have the equivalent of a lesson every day with each class they take; only mathematics teachers are likely to have so many, at least in the early secondary years, before the curriculum narrows to prepare for public examinations. Such teachers have more time to win the trust of their pupils in spite of the secondary school timetable which 'fragments personal relations as surely as it fragments knowledge'. [5] More directly than mathematics teachers, English teachers must find that their objectives bear on the pupils as individuals with emotional as well as intellectual lives. As the HM Inspectorate have recently asserted,

> Good teaching of English, at any level, is far more than the inculcation of skills; it is an education of the intellect and the sensibility. [6]

The central concerns of pupils are inescapably involved as teachers seek to promote qualities in speech, listening, writing and reading which cannot be disentangled from the quality of personal life. The HMIs face the issue, and state it forcibly:

> (Assessment) . . . is inevitably and properly concerned with the quality of what is said — with the depth, validity and perspicacity of the writer's or speaker's thoughts, with the logic of their development, with the aptness and truth of his or her perceptions and the sincerity of his or her feelings. In teaching English we are teaching pupils to think clearly, to be self aware, and to be responsive to their experience of the world of people and things about them. [7]

This dimension of English teaching has concerned Dr Harrison in his earlier publications. In *Learning Through Writing* he warns against an over-emphasis on systematic preparation for public examinations, on mechanical approaches to 'language development' or 'communication skills'. Any useful discussion of 'language development' must respect 'the realm of the growing learning individual'. The actual situation of the young writer must affect our response to a piece of personal writing. A young girl going through a 'time of painful isolation' may show this by the unreal escapism of her story writing; the English teacher has to work 'according to the grain of actual needs, desires, yearnings and imaginings in the growing individual' (*English Studies, 11-18*) and this may mean being prepared to 'wait for the learner's self-responsibility to emerge'. English teachers often accept, even demand, autobiographical writing, and those who share Dr Harrison's views would encourage their pupils to submit for written assignments work which supplements or deviates from set titles and topics. Sarah's letters start in this way, with a long autobiographical piece distantly related to an untimetabled class on *Macbeth*. How should a teacher respond to such a piece of work? It cannot be marked or graded in the conventional way. Has the receiver become a trusted friend receiving a personal confidence, or perhaps a lay therapist collecting material which may form the basis of diagnosis and treatment?

Both pupil and teacher seem to deviate from the roles which they are expected to enact according to the accounts in sociology texts and the orthodoxy of staffroom subcultures. In this uncharted area, a teacher's professional education is unlikely to have been helpful. Dr Harrison was an experienced head of department; but, as he makes clear, the sort of response that he felt appropriate may be severely handled by teachers who take for granted such model definitions of the pupil's role as showing 'industry and drive', 'obedience, punctuality and attentiveness', in conformity with such school mottoes as 'Cheerfulness with Industry'. Even in Sarah's comparatively easy-going comprehensive, the school situation was 'structured to ensure that pupils are continually subjected to pressures underlying these definitions'.[8] Sarah's modest moves to self-assertion — moves a friend might feel she urgently needed to make, such as not conforming to homework requirements, absenting herself from school assemblies, being alone in 'free spaces' rather than sociable in common rooms — were seen as threatening, whereas we should see her resistance to the school's order, for her a disorder, as 'a sign of psychic health'.[9] The social requirements of her school as well as the academic requirements of the A-level treadmill became insufferable to her. And teachers, receiving letters such as Sarah's, exemplify the analysis put forward in a famous paper by Bryan Wilson,[10] that teachers' concern with the whole person must lead to their involvement as a whole person, and that the affective neutrality sought by most professions will not be adequate to support young people seeking 'assurance, support, and a sense of identity'.

The study of recent poetry and fiction is enforced by public examination syllabi, yet one wonders how well understood are the implications of this state of affairs for the role of English teachers. The 'extension of experience and insight' which the HMIs see as a benefit from the study of literature[11] may have uncomfortable consequences for teacher and taught. What can the merely obedient, punctual, attentive pupil, working with an authoritarian teacher, make of Blake or of Lawrence, Orwell or Golding whose disturbing texts are now canonized by examination boards? Was not Lionel Trilling right in seeing a ferocious critique of the 'world taken for granted' as precisely the identifying feature of the modern in literature? His unease in using *The Magic Mountain* as teaching material must be echoed by many English teachers who face the task of bringing about anything more than a sterile encounter of the pupil with the text. After reading *Sons and Lovers* as part of her normal work in English, Sarah chose to continue with *The Rainbow,* not a 'set book'. Surely reading these books must have deepened her trouble in the short term, leading her further from cheerful obedience, punctuality and attentiveness. Lawrence must have encouraged her to devote her intellectual energy to a frighteningly intense self-criticism and deepened her sense of the casual brutality and thoughtlessness of everyday social encounters: 'the depression, the humiliation, the bewilderment of life', as it was perceived by another Henry James character, Peter Sherringham in *The Tragic Muse.*

Through this reading, both required and self-chosen, Sarah more than fulfilled one of the HMIs' objectives for the written work of 16 year olds (alongside 'the ability to compose a curriculum vitae'), that they should write 'clearly and perceptively about personal experiences and their response to them'.[12] Yet the clarity and perception which she achieved led her to abort the sacred A-levels and leave school altogether.

* * *

The story ends happily. Sarah's growing confidence and security owed much to her friends of her own age — but also to the patient concern of her English teachers, the 'concern that appears naturally when one person is interested in another's being'. Sarah could trust that they would 'listen to her and respond to her with seriousness and respect'.[13] In responding like this, rather than claiming professional authority or expertise, they were in accord with the insights of such psychotherapists as Peter Lomas, to whom Dr Harrison introduces us. Lomas develops the view that the paradigm for psychotherapy is 'friendship rather than the application of scientific theory'; 'non-technical qualities are central to healing'.[14] His work should encourage the many teachers who wish to cope responsibly with pupils' emotional problems. And Sarah was greatly helped by a perhaps casual remark from Dr Harrison's colleague[15] on the necessity of being two-faced, a view he might not wish to maintain too seriously. It was what she needed to hear just then. So untidy and unpredictable is human growth.

References

1. P.W. Jackson, *Life in Classrooms*. Eastbourne: Holt, Rinehart and Winston, 1968, p.4.

2. R. Walden and V. Walkerdine, *Girls and Mathematics: From Primary to Secondary Schooling,* Bedford Way Papers 24, University of London Institute of Education, 1985, pp.75-6.

3. Ursula K. Le Guin, *The Wind's Twelve Quarters*. London: Gollancz, 1981, p.94.

4. Simone Weil, 'Reflections on the right use of school studies' in *Waiting on God*. London: Fount Paperbacks, 1977 edn., p.75.

5. T. Dunsbee and T. Ford, *Mark My Words*. London: Ward Lock Educational, 1980, p.13.

6. Department of Education and Science, *English from 5 to 16,* Curriculum Matters 1, an HMI series, para. 3.2. London: HMSO, 1984.

7. Ibid. para. 4.6.

8. M.D. Shipman, *The Sociology of the School,* 2nd edn. Harlow: Longman, 1975, p.54.

9. T. Roethke, epigraph to P.W. Jackson, op.cit.

10. B.R. Wilson, 'The teacher's role, a sociological analysis', *British Journal of Sociology,* Vol.13, 1962, p.26.

11. Department of Education and Science op. cit., para. 1.6.

12. Ibid., p.11.

13. P. Lomas, *The Case for a Personal Psychotherapy.* Oxford University Press, 1981, pp.26, 75.

14. Ibid. pp.6, 7.

15. See p71. below.

1.
Introduction

. . . and when one is honest, there is the horror of confronting one's own void, which must double for the source of fertility, creativity and love. What results is a spiral of delusion and anxiety, networked with enough talent and satisfaction in *technique* that one continues, always hopeful of vision, of compassion, of inspiration. Despite my tone, I believe this; I believe that trying to cope with oneself, even the most bumbling self, in form, may be one aid to self-recovery.

Joyce Hohlwein, in *Touchstones:*
Letters between Two Women, 1953-1965
by P.F. Lamb and K.J. Hohlwein, 1984

Problems of shyness or lack of self-assertion in learners are endemic in schools. Inevitably, these problems do not attract the same attention as those of overt rebellion, yet they may be just as damaging to learning processes. Moreover, this is an 'equal opportunities' issue, since there is evidence that girls are more at risk than boys of being disadvantaged through shyness, and that children in ethnic minority groups may be similarly vulnerable. How can learners be encouraged to help themselves towards greater self-confidence? The question has many aspects, including teachers' attitudes, parents' attitudes and the self-attitudes of learners. This study concentrates on self-attitudes, and on the possibilities of self-help. It dwells briefly on some general principles of self-encounter in learning, in order to introduce a critical account of an adolescent girl's experience in self-encounter, based on a series of letters written by her. The study is intended to be of practical use to teachers who are alert to problems of shyness in their classrooms, and who are aware that some enhanced form of teacher-learner relationship is needed to overcome these. The importance of personal discourse, and especially of personal writing, is emphasized. It is argued that to encourage such writing is by no means to encourage egocentricity or solipsism but, rather, to draw on the benefits of an essential creative process, in which all people can be engaged. For such perceiving (and self-perceiving) is in itself a creative act, linking the ordinary perceptions of our daily living with the rarer perceptions, and the healing qualities, of realized art.

In order to determine some principles for 'self-encounter' insights will be drawn partly from the literary arts, but mainly from the field of psychotherapy. It should be acknowledged that to introduce such insights is to risk entanglement in a still disputed area. Teachers may feel cautious about that area of overlap between the (pedagogical) concerns of teaching, and the (healing) concerns of therapy. One objection here — and one not to be taken lightly — would be that to encourage self-encounter as a kind of therapy, as well as a way of growth, is to risk a form of interference with the individual; that rather than intrude into the learner's private realms, it may be better to ignore them altogether. Yes, it would be an impertinence to attempt to stir up disturbances in another's mind; but it may be a further kind of limiting, perhaps, to refuse to admit that self-stirrings do in any case take place, which schools can hardly ignore if they want to be in touch with the real concerns of children. It is part of my case to suggest that long-established findings in dynamic psychology have much to offer teachers who are concerned with enhancing the quality of classroom relations, and who wish to remove all that is needlessly raw and abrasive from school life.

This need not mean even more work for the already overloaded teacher; for workers in dynamic psychology — Maslow, Bowlby, Winnicott, Guntrip, Lomas among them — concur in emphasizing the primary importance of non-interference with their clients. Their clinical findings show that if we wish to encourage self-discovery, we need usually play no more than the modest role of a listener. Donald Winnicott argued (in *Playing and Reality,* 1971) that there is an essential art in learning *not* to intervene; the listener/counsellor can work from a principle that the answers to the learner's problems invariably lie within the experience of the learner, and wait to be told to a trusting audience.

Few teachers would deny that they ought to find time to listen to learners with problems — personal, emotional, domestic — which have come to affect, even to disable, learning progress. Such time tends to be in too short supply during the busy day of a comprehensive school; but learners with personal difficulties cannot lightly be handed over to clinics, or even to professional teacher-counsellors, in the hope that the learner/patient can be 'conditioned' back to 'normal' behaviour. Such a misconception of counselling was refuted by the psychologist David Smail ('Learning in psychotherapy', 1980); Smail argues against 'scientism' in psychology, and pleads for a more genuinely 'scientific' appreciation of psychotherapy 'as a process of personal learning . . . an active process in which, through his relations with others and with the world, he changes himself. In psychotherapy, the patient changes himself, at least partly through his relation with the therapist.' Smail recognizes an overlap in the roles of teacher and counsellor, in that both need to work from loving regard for the 'otherness' of the learner, from respect for the other's being, and the potential to grow (see also Smail, 1978). The individual's growth towards self-reliance can be helped only through such relationship; where schools are concerned, this is best done through the work-in-progress of a school classroom. Counselling which is separate from the curriculum makes both counselling and curriculum less effective for the learner.

Need for autonomy and need for intimacy

> I speak now of the real self, as the central inner force, common to all human beings and yet unique to each, which is the deep source of growth.

> Karen Horney, *Neurosis and Human Growth,* 1950

Karen Horney held that inner efforts to express feeling might be regarded as positive attempts by the growing individual to meet, and to grow within, the world. The learner needs space for this, in order to enjoy a sense of inner freedom. Karen Horney's terms of definition for the 'real' self drew on the work of Jung, and in turn influenced the thinking, practice and writings of succeeding therapists. A full historical review of the concept of the 'real' self in this century would need to include an account by Freud, Jung, Karen Horney, Melanie Klein, and Michael Fairbairn. This is not within my present scope, but the contribution of three therapists to this area since 1960 — Harry Guntrip, Donald Winnicott and Peter Lomas — bears particularly on the notion of self-encounter and the quality of learning and teaching relations in schools.

In *Schizoid Phenomena: Object Relations and the Self* (1968), Guntrip dwelled on the plight of the schizoid individual, who suffers the distress of isolation in the loss of relations, yet who also fears being smothered by relationships that *do* seem possible in life. Guntrip's view was that the suffering endured by the schizoid individual is potentially everyone's, given unfavourable enough conditions. Even strong identities become precarious under stress (in some cases because they have become firm to a point of inflexibility, their strength has become their weakness), as may be evidenced by the vulnerability of most of humanity to the brain-washing techniques and psychological high-pressure methods used by military governments, political, religious and commercial organizations, as well as at more local and individual levels.

Guntrip defined a nervous breakdown as a self-protecting version of apparent psychic collapse, when the strains of living force individuals to 'shut out the external world and maintain our right to an inviolable privacy within ourselves' in order to retain some remnant inner sense of health, at least. Nervous breakdown is a kind of fail-safe action which operates to protect individuals against being 'psychologically flooded by alien invading experiences' (or, as Winnicott put it, to defend the mind from suffering the 'frightening reality of being infinitely exploited'). Yet the defensive action of self-withdrawal immediately presents individuals with a further dilemma; instead of being invaded, they are now isolated, 'left to flounder in a vacuum'. The courage must somehow be restored to seek again for trusting connection with others, with the world. Guntrip summed up the basic needs of each being, as requiring first an 'inner core' of individuality, and second, a 'still deeper ultimate core' which gives the experience of 'at-oneness' with the world. It is this which generates separate individuality, yet it is 'hard for individuals in our culture to realize that true independence is rooted in and only grows out of primary dependence'. (Guntrip, 1968). In trying to avoid 'invading' the feelings of another, it is not enough simply to leave those feelings to the isolated self of dependent individuals (learner/client/child/friend), to 'flounder in a vacuum'. If we as teachers wish to help, then we have to learn how to provide the support, but not the intrusion, of our ordinary, real selves. If the teacher finds the courage (and the accompanying skill) to provide this, the learner may find space for self-confidence to grow within.

Guntrip urged that an integrating of the need-for-autonomy and of the need-to-relate provided the most assured basis for psychic well-being. He paid tribute to Fairbairn here, who qualified Freud significantly, in showing how all the known forms of mental distress are attributable to the schizoid state, as outlined above. The problem with his clients, stated Guntrip, was often to find ways of enabling them to realize that they were not the 'strong-but-bad' people they assumed themselves to be (which was the view of humanity that Freud tended to affirm, in following the patriarchal patterns of his own culture even where his own insights sought to contradict them). Rather than this, they needed a converse strength that can admit weakness. At heart, claimed Guntrip, we are not heartless, sex-obsessed monsters (or naked apes) who need to repress our outrageous demands on our environment and on each other; but we do have a sometimes overwhelming libidinal need for interrelationship, through which our hunger, power and sex drives ought the more safely to operate. Guntrip emphasizes that 'the basic problem in psychopathology [is] the schizoid problem of feeling a nobody, of never having grown to adequate feeling of real self. If we go far enough, it always emerges in some degree from behind the classic conflicts.'

Among many examples of the 'shut-in' individual who has adopted a set of inflexible routines to avoid living engagement with the world, Guntrip describes how a headmaster-patient came to lose all interest in his school and career, feeling 'totally cut off' from the people in his charge, after fulfilling his life's ambition to secure a headship. He had come to feel love as a dangerous, unpredictable force; instead he sought the safety of, and became himself victim to, rigid routine. The sheer drudgery of 'helping' other people without having his heart in it (he could generate neither love nor hate) drove him to despair at the loss of his very will to live. He had assumed a mechanized, robot personality — had become more a fixed system than a changing person — in his barren efforts to 'help without feeling', without taking the risk of offering his own bodily, loving presence. Guntrip provides many studies of the plight of those who cannot enter into emotional relations with others, except through projection of their own needs or suffering. These accounts of such wasted living — shifting away from friends, from marriage, work, sexual joy, in order to avoid the stress of opening and commitment to another, through the whole spectrum of joy and woe — make sad reading. Yet his is a positive concern — both for the regenerating of individuality and for renewal of a sense of primal connection. While there can be no doubt that these concerns are not new (they are embedded for all to find in *Oedipus,* or *King Lear,* or Rembrandt, or Mahler's music), the case-studies by Guntrip have value in showing how general principles may have a particular application for the professional concerns of therapy and of teaching.

Guntrip discloses how his teacher Fairbairn 'stressed in private conversation that trouble arises not only over the child's needs for the parents, but also over the parents' pressures on the child, who is often exploited in the interests of the parents' needs . . .' Similar dangers are just as present in the learner-teacher relationship, for teachers may reflect the sometimes exploiting attitudes of the wider community (for example, 'we need more computer engineers/commercial designers, etc . . .') as well as their own sometimes exploiting individual motives ('this class will do the creative work *I* require . . .'). And if, through self-inspection, they are made aware of such complications in themselves, they may force inhibitions on themselves in their dealings with learners, both as parents or teachers. In guarding against intrusion, they may become afraid of their own feelings of self-hatred (defined by Guntrip as 'anti-libidinal ego' in his overall concept of self) as they become more aware that these exist; and they may conclude that it is better to avoid feeling-contact altogether, especially with adolescent learners, lest they do harm.

It is not uncommon, even in the recently more relaxed atmosphere of many secondary schools, for a young teacher to be advised to 'keep your distance' from a class, since experience tells that it can be difficult to keep in harmonious touch with a class of young learners. There may be wisdom in such advice, in so far as it reflects how difficult it can be to avoid confounding a suitably protective approach with possessive or interfering attitudes. But too often the advice can merely be a dampener on the young teacher's natural (and, for both teacher and learner, potentially valuable) desire for sincere relationship in the classroom. Schools have, through long-established custom rather than through any cause in basic human make-up, tended to repress the intimacy that could enhance teaching-learning relationships. Every new teacher has to experience the neurosis of the system on joining, and some cope 'better' (in both a true and false sense) with it than others. But virtually none will have received guidance, in training, on the *self*-awareness they will need, in order successfully to offer something rather better than just 'keeping your distance' from the learner. Close association with young learners can make enormous demands on a teacher, and these become unbearable when we are unsure of ourselves, when we are reminded too forcibly of parts of ourselves that have not yet grown up; of opportunities we may have missed; of unresolved problems in our earlier living — all of which we may be tempted to 'put right' in fantasy only, through a possessive relationship; or we may unconsciously deny to the young what may have been denied to ourselves.

Yet intimacy often requires a relaxing, a simple letting-go, rather than yet more effort. Guntrip describes how during the course of analysis a father came to change his attitude towards his small son; at first the father was angrily intolerant whenever the boy cried, but gradually he became more gentle, through recalling his own fears of crying before his father, when he had been a child. Eventually he achieved a fully forbearing patience when his son cried, sharing his sorrow and assuring him that the distress would soon be forgotten. In venturing nearer to his son, and accepting the fact of his distress, the father came into touch with himself, aware now of how he himself had been treated; through allowing the boy to express feeling he came to find room for the expression of his own. This capacity for intimate tolerance (taking the burden, as well as allowing space) of another's feeling is a mark of worthwhile relationships — as parents, as teachers, in public life.

In an essay on 'Education and Culture' (1967) Tolstoy declared with vehemence (he was involved in a dispute with the central educational authorities at the time) that 'Education is the tendency of one man to make another just like himself . . . the feeling of envy raised to a principle or theory.' To counter this, Tolstoy advocated a heuristic approach in learning and teaching, in order to defend children from those who envied their innocence. Here he may take too black-and-white a view of learning, though it reflects the inspiring qualities of good teachers, such as are evident in Tolstoy's own accounts of his teaching experiences at Yasnaya Polyana (1967). It also points to a truth about adult-child relationships which Tolstoy himself revealed, for instance through his picture of Karenin's conflict over studies with his son Seriozha, in *Anna Karenina*.[1] Shakespeare dramatizes such possessive-envious exploiting of a child in *The Winter's Tale,* where Leontes is split between ugly fantasies about his wife's seeming impurity ('it is a bawdy planet') and possessive idealizing of his son Mamillius. He names him 'my captain', 'my collop' and demands pre-rehearsed 'correct' answers from his 'squire' — which his shy, apparently tongue-tied son obediently renders, in monosyllables. Leontes asks his friend and fellow-king Polixenes about his own son; in contrast Polixenes shows (for the present) a free affection, without Leontes' insistent claiming. Polixenes also acknowledges a greater awareness of his own potential afflictions as he moves towards middle age:

> And in his varying childness cures in me
> Thoughts which would else thick my blood . . .,

But Leontes betrays his incomprehension of Polixenes' drift in replying curtly:

> So stands this squire offic'd with me.

Mamillius talks more freely with his mother, who invites him to tease her; but he dies early in the play, when his mother is removed from his life. Polixenes himself comes into conflict with his son later, when the young man finds the strength to exert self-will against his father's prejudice, by marrying the lowly yet truly 'real/royal' Perdita. As with Cordelia in *King Lear,* it is the father's love which has given the child the strength to rebel on behalf of his own life; through love of Perdita the son, Florizel, learns to cross a royal father's will without destruction, thus restoring the authority of loving as opposed to domineering relationships in the court.

The 'thickening' of blood to which Polixenes admits is caused not by natural ageing processes, but by failure to grow within the time of a lifespan; eventually, the play emphasises more the restorative possibilities than the damaging processes of Time. Yet it may be impossible altogether to avoid possessive or envious feelings at deeper levels — especially, as Polixenes discovers, when the demands of the young, maturing adult for release from protection come to be felt as threatening to the world 'we' have built. The parent/teacher needs to find new resources of patience, flexibility and generosity to allay those tragic elements that remain inherent in relations between old and young.

Most costly to the 'mature' adult, perhaps, is finding the courage to admit personal frailties; yet it is Guntrip's view that this is a fundamental requirement for well-being. Guntrip offers a qualification of Ian Suttie's (1935) notion of the 'taboo on tenderness', in advancing that 'the real taboo is on weakness', so that distorted patterns of domination extend even into love-making itself. Given the external pressures on our schools (for example, through the examination system) it is hardly surprising that teachers might experience, more than most, the burden of ensuring that they and the young whom they teach should be 'strong' in competence externally, and that the 'weak' side of themselves and their learners should tend to become associated 'only' with their 'subjective' selves, into which any 'weakness' might be conveniently (if temporarily) driven. Yet any school which places external conformity (in curriculum, in rules, in learning patterns) before respect for the individual humanness of its teachers and learners can only have evil effects, whatever its declared 'ideals' or 'standards', by conspiring to consign any weakness of selfhood to the imprisonment of a split-off 'inner' self. Schooling needs a movement towards mutuality of recognition among teachers and learners; for when that contact is avoided, both the learner's and the teacher's need for relationships, without which there is no real growth of being for learner or teacher, are denied. Furthermore, when the 'weaknesses' of our underdeveloped or distorted selves are admitted, a stronger self-trust is achieved. In frailty, by paradox, lies the way to strength. When challenging the mind-body split of Descartes' 'cogito ergo sum', Guntrip suggested,

'A natural human being would be more likely to start from, "I *feel, therefore I am*".' This might be taken a stage further, to 'I love, therefore I am', since the admitting of feeling depends on self-acceptance and acceptance of others.

The 'good enough' adult

In *Schizoid Phenomena*, Guntrip dwelled on the problem of admitting the presence of our seeming 'weak' real self, and of coping with its weaknesses. Donald Winnicott, whose work has been influential on educationists, tended to place rather more emphasis on the robustness of the individual who has been given what he termed a 'good enough' start in life, through a 'good-enough' primal mother-child relationship. We are indebted to Winnicott for his clarification of the notions of 'real' self and 'false' self, in writings that reflected his long career of clinical work with children.

Basic to Winnicott's thought was his notion of a 'play-area' or 'potentially creative space' (*Playing and Reality,* 1971), between the individual growing child and the person/object with which the child seeks relationship; it is this space which becomes filled with the 'products of the baby's own creative imagination'. In the search for vital relationship, the child may be fulfilled or failed by parent-figures in the quality of provision of this 'play-area', for the child who 'adopts an object as almost part of the self could not have adopted it unless it had been lying round for adoption'. Making things available for children, he declared, is not to be confounded with imposing things on them, either by trying directly to 'implant morals' (for example, insisting on 'cleanliness' in rigid sphincter control in the early stages, or on belief in a particular version of God later on); nor is it to be confused with a wholesale refusal to choose on behalf of the child, like the father who

> refused to allow his daughter to meet any fairy story, or any idea such as that of a witch or a fairy or a prince, because he wanted his child to have only a personal personality; the poor child was being asked to start again with the building up of the ideas and artistic achievement of the centuries. This scheme did not work . . .
>
> *The Maturational Processes and the Facilitating Environment,* 1965

Children depend on provision in order to learn; without stories, allegories, homilies, histories, as well as their direct experience, they have no correlative for their own intuitions, dark or light. Winnicott offers a distinction here between personal achievement and implant; between the adult as a providing and reassuring presence, and the adult as restricting director and manipulator; between growth towards individual maturing, and 'unreal' success based on a compliance with outside demands at the expense of inner needs. The worst immorality that the infant can suffer is 'to comply at the expense of the personal way of life'. Inner needs cannot 'successfully' be ignored, and any attempt to do so exposes the growing individual even to moral disintegration. It becomes clear that to accept Winnicott's argument is to accept also that the quality of *what* we teach, what we choose to make available to the 'play-area', or 'potentially creative space' of the learner, will be crucial to the quality of his/her becoming — as will our modes of presentation, and of relating to the learner. The quality of the curriculum is bound up with the quality of teacher-learner relationships, and vice-versa; neither can be isolated from the other.

Along with his recognition of the learner's need for 'potentially creative space' Winnicott acknowledges, too, that the parent-figure can never abdicate from providing and sharing a full give-and-take relationship with the learner. In a final chapter, called 'Contemporary Concepts of Adolescent Development', he matched his earlier stress on the importance of space for the growing individual with an anti-sentimental statement on the importance of not confounding the real needs of adolescents with self-assertions about what they think they need. While they need to make assertions of their needs, these are not to be taken just at face value:

> While growing is in progress, *responsibility must be taken by parent-figures* [author's italic]. If parent-figures abdicate, then the adolescent must make a jump to a false maturity and lose their greatest asset: freedom to have ideas and act on impulse . . . Confrontation must be *personal*. Adults are needed if adolescents are to have life and liveliness . . . Where there is the challenge of the growing boy or girl there let an adult meet the challenge. And it will not necessarily be nice. In the unconscious fantasy these are matters of life and death.

> *Playing and Reality* (1971)

The emphasis here contrasts with but does not contradict Guntrip; both recognize the need for reliable, self-trusting adults who know enough of themselves to be able to offer appropriate support to the young. In learning to trust themselves more as adults, and to take on creative relationship with the young, adults may come to release themselves from their own destructive, compulsive fears; they may be able to offer the support which the young need to cope with their own pains of growth, and the inevitable losses that accompany growth.

Winnicott helped the teacher to recognize that the capacity for maturing lies in the learner, who is *naturally* capable of building a realistic grasp of his world, through 'good enough' primal relationships. The growing is the learner's growing, although it depends for its quality on good provision from the learning environment. Thus the teacher's skill will lie largely in making provisions to which the learner in turn can *choose* to relate. Also, the teacher has a duty to offer a resistance in relationship; there must be no abdication from meeting the *challenge* of the young. This is not to justify possessive or authoritarian (Leontes-like) patterns, but to acknowledge that teachers need to be strong in themselves, in order to be able to match adolescent challenge with adult reliability, to ensure a creative partnership on both sides.

True and false versions of reality
Peter Lomas's work (1973, 1981) deserves the attention of teachers who do not have specific psychological or medical training, in that he placed emphasis, not on any particular clinical method of approach or set of skills needed, but on the ordinary person-to-person aspects of any relationship, including that of the therapist-patient. In books that are free of the specialist jargon of psychology and psychotherapy, he affirmed that any relationship, personal or professional, needs to be a shared experience. He recommended that we remove any sense in the other person that he is 'special' in any way, even though he may, for the time being, 'have lost the capacity for ordinary living'. It is best to avoid rigid postures of pupil/teacher, boss/worker, parent/child, since 'a harmful inequality between parent and child leads to false ways of experiencing life' (*True and False Experience,* 1973). Like Guntrip, Lomas urged that we admit our own 'frailty', even though (as in the case of teaching) a rather special kind of relationship is being offered — 'a relationship in which one person helps another to grow'. This book is prefaced with a reflection from Malraux: 'And then, the fundamental fact is, there is no such thing as a grown-up person.' The therapist/teacher may take comfort that in seeking greater self-awareness and skill in helping others, and while seeking to offer on the whole a decent normality, there need be no pretence to be an infallible source of wisdom; for there is more of the child (in both child-like and child-ish aspects) in the adult than adults usually care to admit.

Like Winnicott, Lomas showed concern for the child's view of things, and the need for play and bodily touch in older lives. Lomas found through his own work with clients that when relationships are conducted on a basis of simple, ordinary respect for individuals, without the intervention of 'harmful inequalities', then the other partner in the relationship may feel that he is 'valued for his ordinary human qualities, those which he shares with the rest of mankind: fundamentally, his capacity to experience'. Lomas's emphasis here, that *all* relationships should be on this basis, is radical; it links him in this respect to the better known work of R.D. Laing, especially where parent/child relationships are concerned. Indeed, Lomas pays generous tribute to Laing; but he also makes what he regards as a fundamental criticism of Laing's outlook, in that rather than discerning potentially ordinary being behind schizoid behaviour, Laing saw the acting-out of such distress itself as being evidence of a 'superior being'. Lomas held that Laing's detection of an error in counselling ('bow down to your guide') led him to an equally dangerous abstraction ('be governed by your fantasies'). This is a telling criticism of Laing's position; it reinforces, too, that subjectivity can only be truly identified within a relationship; as far as schools are concerned, this involves the teacher-learner relationship.

Concerning the growth of the real self, Lomas offered a useful classifying of two major and related areas of damage which may be suffered by the growing individual. First, there are experiences which diminish children's belief in their own capacity and worth; second, there are experiences which diminish children's belief in the capacity of others to respond to and care for them. The first experience can lead to an excessive parasitic dependence on parent-figures, while the second leads to a false independence, where the child despairs of finding trust or intimacy in relationship. If we wish to be helpful agents, it is likely that a quick respect for the 'otherness' of the client will be a more valuable basis than possession of out-of-context counselling 'skills'. For Lomas, the kind of relationship needed for good therapy envisages 'technique' in the service of a strong sense of common humanity, and a respect for the other's identity. The person who is offering help must be an ordinary human being; it is in the acknowledgement of this ordinariness that one's sense of 'frailty' lies. Full recognition of the other person requires, moreover, a more than residual 'kindness', or 'humanness'; only the removal of harmful inequalities (for example, between teacher and learner) will enable the removing of false relationships, false ways of experiencing life, and a restored sense of one's own, personal 'normality'. The teacher needs a special alertness in order fully to imagine the needs of the other, the learner-in-difficulty. There are skills to be learned, but these skills in helping other people to grow (as offered by teachers, parents, therapists, friends) are rooted in love, rather than in 'a body of doctrine'. A sense of both the 'ordinariness' and the individuality of both self and the other are specially required. Concerning the nurture of the real self (from which 'true experience' is felt), if the real self is hurt, self-trust and a sense of meaning in life is hurt too. In extreme cases, there is even a loss of will to live. Lomas declares, too, that in dealing with the real self of a child, we are dealing with the actual life, and even the risk of death, in the individual.

Teachers enter willy-nilly into a human relationship with the learner; they cannot decently evade the responsibilities that grow from the commitment of any ordinary relationship between one human being and another. Writing on learning relationships, Marjorie Hourd suggested:

> For some time we have recognized the importance of the teacher-child relationship as a factor in learning, but we are only just beginning to understand that if the teacher is to put himself in the right position with children he must be in contact with the child in himself. This is something rather different from being 'child-like' and 'interested in' children. Sometimes, in fact, child-study can be a way of avoiding the claims of the child inside, by focusing attention on the one in the classroom. But knowing what it is to be a child, by coming to terms with the child in ourselves, is knowledge of another kind because it involves recognizing the aggressive roots of personality, as well as the more benign sources of influence.
>
> *Relationship in Learning,* 1972

Majorie Hourd's reference to the 'claims of the child inside', and to the 'aggressive' as well as 'benign' sources of growth, reminds the teacher that the task on behalf of shy learners is to restore vital contact between them, their fellow-beings and their world. The proper aim is towards more free, confident, friendly and simple relationships with those whom we teach. Teaching and learning — even when the age gap is wide, as is common in schools — is at best collaborative, a human adventuring. And since, as in any genuine relationship, the respect given and received has an unconditional basis, it is inevitable that sometimes more of ourselves will be demanded than may be fitted into any comfortably stereotyped or expedient version of the teacher's role. The case study that follows concerns itself with just such a demand, made by a fifteen-year-old girl, who 'wrote herself' through a personal crisis. Her account was essentially a singular experience; but it is representative of the experience of many learners, in depicting what it is like to reach out to one's own adulthood.

I feel stronger now than I have ever felt in the last six years. Perhaps I appear a weak person to a lot of people but, I know, that I am not so weak. I admit I am rather soft and easily hurt but other people cannot sway me when I really believe something. I think I have become stronger because I feel more confident in myself and I think David and Richard have helped me a lot. People have often avoided laughing at me openly, for fear of hurting me, and although at the time I was grateful, I now realise it hindered me because I always took myself and other people seriously. I could never laugh at myself because, I felt so self-conscious and inhibited that I couldn't bear any form of criticism, even if it was only a joke. I didn't even feel annoyed, just hurt. If a person criticised me I used to force a laugh, but inside I felt as if I had been stabbed. Beneath the cover the wound bled painfully. What the person said would keep going through my mind, again and again, until I was numbed by the pain. I suppose lack of confidence has always prevented me from laughing at myself. When you feel uncertain and insecure, it is very difficult to accept criticism, because this makes you feel even less sure of yourself and other people. If I was criticised I felt the person disliked me or was trying to get at me in some way, which was stupid of me I suppose, but as I said in my other essay,

2
The Case Study

> . . . Am I right in thinking that we said that a top-ranking craftsman . . .
> in any field must be able not merely to concentrate on the many, but to
> press on to knowledge of the one, and in the light of that knowledge to
> organize all his details with a total 'synoptic' view . . ?
>
> Plato, *The Republic*

Sarah's writing took the form of a series of letters, written to her English
teachers over a period of some eighteen months, during her fifth and sixth
years in a comprehensive school. In these letters she attempted a sustained
self-probing account of her state of feelings during that time. A total of
sixteen letters survived (around twenty thousand words in all) which
represented only about half of those actually written; these were the ones
that I myself had retained. Others had been handed back, sometimes with
written comments on them; when she was approached for permission to
quote from and discuss the letters, she revealed that she had lately
destroyed her own collection prior to her marriage, as being part of a now
closed chapter in her life. She gladly agreed that the surviving letters might
be used for this study.

Autumn term: fifth year
The first letter in this series came just before Christmas in her fifth year.
She was one of a small, self-selected group who were studying *Macbeth*
outside normal school and lesson hours, in preparation for O-level. Her
writing was offered as a substitute for some work that I had set the group
on the play. This was not in itself unusual, but it was Sarah's first attempt
since I had known her (from the beginning of the fourth year), to write
directly about herself. She had previously kept to the text, opting

to write long descriptive accounts of books she had read, where she revealed close involvement with the 'other' world of the author. This first letter was prompted by a particular lesson, although it had not been remarkable; the pupils still seemed to be quite enjoying their reading and discussions of the play, though we were easing off as Christmas approached. We had looked at the opening of the second Act, where Banquo, with his son Fleance, meets Macbeth in the pitch-black of night outside the castle. After some initial guardedness, Banquo meets Macbeth with open friendship, and tells him how he has left Duncan 'shut up in measureless content' in Macbeth's castle. Banquo wants to talk of his dreams and to share his thoughts about the 'wierd sisters' with Macbeth; but Macbeth breaks off the conversation — 'I think not of them', he says — yet we know that he is lying. Macbeth goes on to speak with strange, tense innuendos, inviting his former friend to 'cleave to my consent'; but Banquo, now thoroughly on his guard, replies cautiously, warning Macbeth that he will 'keep my bosom franchised and allegiance clear' in seeking honours. The class had recalled the earlier description of Macbeth — 'rapt' round in his own musings, in his inner fantasies of kingship, the 'swelling act of the imperial theme', no longer in touch with his friends, with other realities. Macbeth cannot find the art to persuade Banquo to share his increasingly dangerous fantasies; he can only withdraw from open, sincere contact. The group had been asked to write on this Macbeth-Banquo encounter; to develop it into a discussion on friendship, if they chose, both in their experience and in the play. Other possibilities for writing were discussed too.

Sarah's contribution, returned several days late, was her first (very long) letter, where she claimed that she did not care if she was 'in trouble' for not doing what was 'set', but she 'had to' write as she had done. (Yet she well knew that there had never been 'trouble' when the class took their own directions in writing. In any case, the class had primed me against becoming over-excited about homework, by their often related tale of a frightening moment with a previous teacher, who had smashed a glass on the desk in his rage over unreturned homework, and then dared them, by gorgonizing them, to 'notice' that his hand was bleeding on the cut glass.)

Sarah's letter was the kind which insisted that whoever read it should take some notice of the writer; belatedly, I began to reconsider my view of her as a hardworking, shy and seemingly colourless pupil. Until then I had known other members of her family better than her. Like all her family, Sarah was physically small; she seemed extremely timid, never saying anything in class. She had always worked well in her reading and writing. She would sit apparently happily enough, if quietly, on the fringe of a small group of more robustly cheerful girls who seemed to show a somewhat maternal affection for her.

Her first letter provided an introduction to her background. Painstakingly written and skilfully shaped, it gave details of her family, neighbourhood and schooling to date. She came from a close family, with two older girls and three younger boys. Those of secondary school age were all at our school. Her father, a skilled craftsman, and her mother, a nurse, both found time to support our evening English department 'open' meetings, film shows and discussions for parents. The parents showed a close, though not possessive, sense of protection for their children. the oldest girl (mentioned frequently in Sarah's letters) was a talented painter, who eventually won a scholarship to an art college; it looked as though Sarah might shine in more conventional academic progress, and go to university to read English or Languages. She had been transferred to the comprehensive school (at her own and her family's request) from a local grammar school, where she had been considered to be a conscientious pupil by her former teachers, though not achieving as well as she should there; they claimed that her weakness in maths should have barred her from 11-plus success in the first place. She was now with the same children who had come with her older sister from the small backstreet secondary school, to form the nucleus of the new comprehensive school.

During her early teens, her father had changed from being a working craftsman to being a trade union representative, which resulted in their moving from a council house to a suburban private-estate, white-collar area. This involved Sarah and her family in an important uprooting; the social changes were confusing for her, seeming to work in both ways at once:

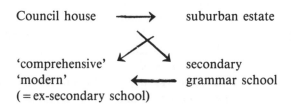

She described the impact of these changes:

When I went to the grammar school my confidence in my academic abilities was destroyed. I would have had a lack of confidence anyway because I am that sort of person but it would not have been as bad as what it was. I had wanted to be a teacher so far back as I can remember and my hope had never faltered until I went to the grammar school. I had believed I had the ability to become a teacher, I loved children and I was reasonably intelligent; or so I thought. My hopes were shattered. That school convinced me I was ignorant, and stupid to have even hoped of becoming a teacher. Exam after exam low marks and I felt desperate even though I was never bottom in the class. However hard I worked my results would not go up. I had lost confidence in my ability as a person so I had based my hopes on my intelligence. At twelve and a half years old I cried myself to sleep because I was so frightened I would never pass any 'O' levels and so would not become a teacher. From the time I started the school the teachers were forever cramming my brains with how important the 'O' levels were. I became very serious and worried a great deal about my work and 'O' levels. My sister who was nearly two years older than me never worried about exams and her work. She was not a worrying sort of person anyway but I was and this school did not help me. If anybody asked me what I wanted to be when I left school I would never say a teacher because I thought they would laugh at me for having such high hopes. Deep down inside me I still wanted to become a teacher but I refrained from letting anyone know. Even though my exam results were not good my nan still believed I would become a teacher. She never gave up believing in me. I think my dad was rather disappointed although he never actually showed any feelings or disappointment. I felt disappointed in myself for them. I gave up. I did not feel capable of the work and that was that. I stayed away from school as often as I could so that I missed most of the lessons and quite often I would spend lessons in the sick room. The school crushed me a great deal because of the cold strictness and the importance of 'O' levels. As soon as one started the school at eleven years old one was informed of the fact you were at the school to get 'O' levels and that was all. There was my sister, nearly two years older than me and not caring a damn about 'O' levels, exam results or anything. I feel my dad wanted her to care more and was pleased I cared but to me it seems wrong. She was happy; really happy. She has always been wonderful at art and English so they were the only things that mattered to her. She was no good at maths but she did not worry. She used to come home from school and tell my mum all that had happened and what the boys in her class had done. I felt left out. I remember it was 1st April and I was going to tell my mum what some girls in my class had done but after my sister had told my mum what some of the sixth-form boys had done, I felt my story was weak. I suppose it was jealousy but I did want to enjoy myself at school. I wanted to be really good at something at school. My sister was one of the best artists in her school and I was very proud of her but I felt I was hopeless at everything. When my friends were looking at paintings pupils from our school had done I felt frustrated becaused the paintings were not nearly as good as those at her school. People from my school might have been good at maths and science but they did not have a strong creative feeling. I was longing to belong to a school I felt I could care about. Perhaps I would have got better exam marks if I worked harder but I did not want to belong to this school. From the day I started the school till the day I left I despised it. When I sat in assembly each morning I used to look at the sixth formers sitting on the platform and I used to try and understand how they had stayed at the school so many years. Surely they had not enjoyed it, I used to think. I could not believe they were happy. I used to. sit listening to the head mistress, feeling thoroughly sick and alone in my heart. I was sitting amongst seven hundred females and yet I felt alone. Why wasn't anybody else so seriously depressed with the school? But then I did not know what they were thinking; they did not know what I was thinking. The teachers sat along the sides of the hall, they were detached from the pupils. I find it difficult to talk to people anyway, but I never even imagined that there was any possibility of pupils actually talking to the teacher about anything other than their lessons . . .

She went on to describe her varying (mainly unhappy) memories of different lessons in this school, occasionally revealing gratitude for the warmth or freshness of a particular teacher, but more usually admitting her sense of coldness and lack of contact with both teacher and class-members. She reflects on her music lessons:

The girls at my other school sang a lot in assembly and in the music lessons. I never did because I felt self-conscious and embarrassed but I loved to listen to the songs. Up to the third year we did theory mainly in the music lesson and I hated it. In the third year we sang every music lesson. One lesson we sang 'Where 'er you walk'. The only thing that prevented me from feeling contented was the strictness. The wind was whisking the leaves from the trees and ground. The sky was grey and I wanted to be outside so that I could be part of this other world. I wanted to rush out and be blown about. Blown as far away from the school as possible, taking the song with me. I wanted to be with the wind, the greyness and the song. But there I was in a sound proof room. Locked in. I wanted to break out, away from this falsehood, away from everything. I wanted to run to what I loved. Did anyone know how I felt? Did anyone feel the same? An old man clutching his hat and scarf walked by the window, frowning with annoyance. The bell rang for the end of the lesson.

Couldn't this school offer me the warmth I needed? I wanted warmth and a feeling of belonging somewhere but I could not belong to this school, I would not let myself. I wanted to belong to warmth and this school did not have enough to offer me. I suppose I did not offer the school any warmth either.

At the carol service we stood and sat when told, I loved the carols but they only made me feel more desperate. I wanted to run out of the hall and never return, I wanted the carols to be sung by the whole school. I just could not believe the girls were happy and contented with the school. Because I hated the school I felt everybody ought to hate it. Somehow I knew I would not stay at the school. Whatever happened I could not stay there. Teachers were at the school to teach lessons and the pupils were there to learn. There was no intimacy. Single-sexed schools are not good schools anyway. A school which consists of just females is terrible because they tend to be jealous and 'catty'. My school was cold and almost frightening. I was frightened because I felt I was wasting my life.

The coldness surrounded me as I opened the door and stepped in. I shivered and felt sick. I walked along the corridor with its cold, polished floor and I felt I was in a tunnel, walking as if drawn by a magnet. This was the aisle to emptiness and nothing. I wanted warmth and security. I wanted to belong and feel glad I belonged, but not to this school. This was not for me, I was not going to let myself belong to this school. I sometimes felt an onlooker, not part of it. I would sit in the classroom and watch everybody working hard, the teacher sitting at the front. I could not believe this was actually happening. I wanted to wake up and find it had all been a dream.

Day and night I would pretend I lived in another world. The only way I could get to sleep was by thinking until I fell asleep. Even now I can't fall asleep without having thought for a couple of hours. I usually think about when I was a child, or I think about people I know and try to understand them. When I was at the grammar school I was completely evading my life because I felt I could not cope.

Having described her unhappy years in this school, she recalled the closeness of her family life, and how isolated she felt on their moving. Her picture of the old roots is appreciative, but the less attractive details are not suppressed or sentimentalized:

When I started the grammar school we had just moved to the house we live in now. As we had moved from our neighbours and friends I suppose I felt even more lonely. I did feel lonely: more than I had ever felt before. We used to live on a council estate, we had lived there almost eleven years. All the children there had grown up together and so we all played together. Our house was only two bedroomed and was semi-detached. It was untidy but warm. Us five children slept in the largest bedroom. It was terrible really, we had just enough room to walk between the beds, but we usually jumped on the beds to get across the room. Often when we were in bed we would hear the girl next door chasing her younger brother up the stairs and then the slam of a door. The boy was one and a half years older than me and his sister was three years older than him. They and their parents are some of the kindest and most good people I have ever known. They have faults, haven't we all? Every one of them was in the habit of exaggerating and being slightly big-headed but they were not cruel and hard. They never meant any harm by it. I supposed I liked them having so much confidence in themselves because I lacked this and they seemed to give me more confidence. They would do anything for us and I think my mum and dad would do anything for them. I do not think you would meet such good friends anywhere else in the world. My mum and dad would agree with that. My dad and sister were not so close to our neighbours as my mum and me. They preferred their own company. If they were happy like that I am glad but one thing my mum and I have in common is the need for this warmth. My mum misses our neighbours but she has made friends with women who are not snobbish like the women in our road. Truthfully I don't think I want anybody to take the place of my old neighbours. I suppose I won't make the effort but I find it hard to go out so I do not meet people. It is not people of my own age who I lack a warmth from. I have got friends like Sandra and Gill. It is older people. People my mum's age. I do not know why I enjoy this sort of company. I just feel at ease and relaxed. Our neighbours here dislike children and are forever telling my brothers to be quiet when they are playing in the garden. During the summer holidays I was sitting in the garden while my brothers were playing. They were making a noise but it was not very loud. The lady next door was watching them with absolute disgust but as soon as my mum came out into the garden she was all smiles. Why do people want to dislike children? Children mess up the house and garden. Our house is the untidiest house in our part of the road, but what does it matter? My old neighbours loved children. When I was young I used to help my aunt Nell (we called her that) do her housework. Out of the children in my family I was the one who lived in their warmth most. In summer I would come home from school and find my mum sitting in the garden talking to my aunt Nell as they drank their tea. I loved sitting with them and listening to them talking. They might be standing on the doorstep talking to a couple of other women from the estate. I suppose people would say this was wasting time but it wasn't, not to me. It was lovely coming home from school seeing my mum and aunt talking and watching my little brothers playing on the grass in front of the house. They were often laughing and joking. As I turned the corner into my road I could see my mum and aunt. I used to run as fast as I could to get home and see my brothers and mum and dad. It was safer than where we live now. Very few cars came there because the road curved into a circle so you ended up where you had started. There were two greens which we played on and we also had a back garden and a front garden. The front gardens were all open but where we live now people have their gardens boxed in. The top part of our garden was a dump but lovely. We had a little house and a slide which my dad had built for us but they were falling to bits because of age and the rough wear they had suffered. My brothers had dug an enormous hole in the middle of the garden but they had hours of fun digging so my dad decided not to stop them. I think this was very kind of him because I know he would like a really beautiful garden and yet he gave his own pleasure up for my little brothers. Not a lot of parents are so unselfish as my mum and dad.

In the evening my brother Stephen, David and Jackie (the boy and girl from next door) my best friend, myself and a few other children used to go to the heath which joined onto the estate and played rounders or some other game. The air would become quite cool towards 8 o'clock but I did not feel cold, I felt alive. Quite often we played in front of our houses and sometimes on the shed roofs which joined the back gardens. If it was hot we sometimes had picnics of our own on the roof or over the heath. We stayed out playing until it was quite dark because we felt safe, we had plenty of playing space and there were no main roads. My mum and dad did not work so hard as they do now and they joined in the fun with us. Sometimes on Sunday afternoons my dad used to take us over to the part of the heath which was on the other side of the main road. My dad used to chase us among the trees and when he caught us he tickled us. All my friends used to come and really he was like a dad to them as well. They all liked him a lot because he joined in the games with us and we felt he wanted to. We ran amongst the trees and ferns, stained our clothes and getting altogether filthy; but who cared. I loved the trees as they wavered in the wind and the ferns turning golden brown; I loved my dad. My dad did so many things for us I could never write them.

I want my youngest brothers to have this love as well. Ian is eight and Matthew is five. They need more freedom I think. My mum and dad give them freedom but they can't go out to play without an adult because of the main roads. They have toys and things like that but I do not feel children really need all the toys they have. Most boys love running about on heaths or cycling. They cannot make a lot of noise because of neighbours. My mum and dad give my brothers their attention, more than a great many parents give their children but I do not feel it is quite right. My mum and dad are older so really it is not surprising that they are not so patient as they used to be and they have to work very hard. Too hard. My dad does not get enough sleep and rest. When we were small and we asked my dad to play with us he would be pleased to but now he seems to feel while he is playing with my brothers he could be getting on with some work. I hate this because I am sure he wants to spend time with my brothers but all the time he feels there is work to do. I do not see a way out of this problem really because rates and bills have got to be paid but I feel my mum, dad and younger brother spend too much time indoors. My mum is always in the house except when she is shopping. We most probably have arguments because we are all in the house together every minute except when we are at school. Holidays are the worst times. I never go out so we all feel everybody else is in the way. I feel terrible when my brothers are fighting. One is shouting to my mum who is machining upstairs, they fight so cruelly, they seem to hate each other. They are jealous of each other and torment each other terribly; when they have been arguing all day I feel I wish I were dead. Why can't everybody be happier? I know children fight but surely not so viciously, not with so much hatred. I cannot shut the arguing out of my mind, I cannot go up to my bedroom and ignore it, it means too much to me. It should not mean a lot to me but it does. Almost everything means a lot to me whether happy or miserable. My heart aches because the one thing in the world I want is for us to be a happy family.

In acknowledging frustration within her family, she suggests how this has risen from the different pattern of their lives which demands more 'respectability'; from an environment which discourages independent play among the young — they 'must be accompanied by an adult . . .'; and from the growing pressures and demands on her father, which were distancing him from the family at a critical time. Their move 'up' the social ladder has been experienced only as a loss by her, and by her family too, she feels. She develops her sense that she has lost opportunities for independent exploration as she grows up by referring to her rebellious feelings about homework and exams, and a growing sense of confusion about her hopes of becoming a teacher:

Why do I have to know so much maths and pass exams to teach five and six year old children? Surely a person is either suitable or not. Some people who are very kind and could teach small children very well cannot become teachers because they cannot pass 'O' levels. I feel unhappy and angry when I think of teenagers spending out their youth so that they feel there is chance of them having a happy future. I enjoy school work but I want to do it because it means something to me. Homework means nothing to me. I often think I am stupid for doing the homework when I would prefer to do something else. I have not done my homework because I wrote this essay and I will most probably be in trouble but just being able to tell somebody how I feel is more important. This seems to be a terrible time to feel so rebellious towards homework and exams. Before I did my homework and felt relieved it was over. Now I'm going to take exams which will decide whether I'll ever be a teacher or not and I feel like throwing everything in. I think I would if becoming a teacher did not mean so much to me. I enjoy the day at school but quite often people have had enough of that type of work and do not want to do more at home. Personally I don't mind doing more work so long as I have decided upon it myself. It is ridiculous of me to write all this really because I don't suppose it will make any difference. I'll come home from school and do most of my homework. In January and June I will be sitting exams. I will most probably fail over half of them and so will keep on sitting the exams until I pass. All this in hope that I will become a teacher. I may never become a teacher, I can't say I have got much confidence in it. Perhaps I am only against exams because I am frightened of what they will do to my hopes of becoming a teacher. Except for becoming a teacher, I have not got any hopes in the future. That's really why I live in the past. I am not against work, I need to keep my mind active but I just detest the way we are expected to work. I don't know what would take over exams to make things better. I feel I should not have written this essay now because all I do is moan and complain. Do you think I ought to stop thinking about my past? When I lie in bed or even when I am doing my homework I am thinking about something that pleased or upset me quite a few years ago. I know it is my own fault my life is not up to much. I won't go out and do what I really want to do. I'm weak really because I need other people to help make me go out. I need a lot of persuasion and it is wrong of me to want other people to help me. I am like an old woman at fifteen years old. I hoard things I have been given when I was a child, in an old case. I don't want anybody to look in there because although it is only rubbish, it is private and means a lot to me. I don't know why I want to keep it until I die. I hope I die in the country where it is peaceful and beautiful. Perhaps all the country will be destroyed before I die and then I will most probably die beside a large motorway or flyover or in an asylum.

(December, fifth year)

The letter is both self-pitying and angry; sad at the sense of loss, and full of angry criticism of her 'academic-mill' school experiences. Sarah records how she feels swamped by academic routine, and resents having to comply with outside-imposed demands of learning which she is not enjoying at all, mainly because she is, or has been, capable of instructing herself to a considerable degree. Also, and more deeply, she is uneasy about her own life-responses, which have been too exclusively book-bound recently — her own 'inner' motivation is in danger of dying. This, she feels, is partly because of outside-imposed pressure, and also because of her fear of seeking out other choices ('I'm weak really because I need other people to help make me go out . . .'). She senses she has been too compliant, and feels a new need to rebel against this, but fears that she may not be strong enough to move from within. The letter ends sadly and wryly, seeing no way to restore what she clearly sees to have been a great loss to her family, indeed to everybody. This loss is identified as warm, close relationships, relaxed neighbourliness and the happy company of friends. The letter reads almost like a period-piece, nearer perhaps to the kind of account of personal upheaval that Richard Hoggart recorded in *Uses of Literacy* (1957) than to the supposed concerns of a 'teenager in the Space Age'. Sarah had read and been impressed by Lawrence's *Sons and Lovers* during the term, and it is not difficult to detect some debt in her letter to Lawrence's presentation there of family closeness. She had done a good deal of work on the book, almost paraphrasing line for line large parts of it,[2] but this was the first directly personal piece of writing that she had ventured from it.

Spring term, fifth year

With her consent, this letter was published the following term in our school magazine of personal and imaginative writing. It became much discussed in the school; reactions to it in the common room were polarized — some approving, some very hostile. After a few days attempts, ultimately successful, were made to have the magazine withdrawn, because Sarah's article might offend some local bodies (a move which helped to guarantee it a

wider and more careful readership than it might have otherwise expected).
The letter was criticized on the grounds that it was ill-advised to write so
forthrightly about other schools, even if they were not actually mentioned by name; and also, that it was 'depressed and depressing'. This second
charge was substantial; Sarah's preoccupation with unhappy things is expressed in flat tones; it is repetitious, and the ending of the letter seems
worryingly morbid. I had hoped that the article would be a once-and-for-
all writing out of a problem, as was quite often the case among learners
of her age; that she would make a few useful self-adjustments — such
as joining a youth club, perhaps asserting herself more in class, and living a little more outside the confines of her home and school. She might
then be able to add talking to the reading and writing that she had previously enjoyed. But her work in the second term never seemd to take flight,
and she seemed spiritless. She admitted that she was not really enjoying
even her English lessons, for instance, in the way that she had enjoyed
her work on *Sons and Lovers,* in the previous term. That book, she felt,
had represented a crossroads for her; before, she had read books only
to become 'lost' in them, but Lawrence had given her feelings of both
strength and unease; she wanted to admit these new feelings into her living.

Surprisingly she seemed amused and not at all worried by the fuss over
her magazine article, which had been published about half-way through
the second term. I had one or two brief interviews with her after lessons
to tell her what she should know of the facts concerning the dispute, and
she said on one of those that she would like to talk further about the letter
itself. After going over one or two points, she went on to talk about her
day-dreaming as she had described it in the letter. She said in a tone of
some resolve that she no longer wanted to withdraw like that again, it
made her feel 'empty'. Responding to her tacit wish to talk about this,
I asked her what she saw as the difference between actual dreaming and
day-dreaming.

'Well, this empty feeling' she said, and continued to chide herself for
her vacancy and self-pity. I suggested that she should not be too hard on
herself here (a suggestion I came to find myself repeating too often to
her); that her yearning for a 'golden clime' was not all that unusual, was
it? Did not the strongest people have their wistful moments, dreaming
of better times, past and future? She said her father did not talk so much
now about his ideals and hopes; he had made her think he was going to
change things when she was younger.

She asked me if I thought she was odd; I replied that the experiences
described in her letter overlapped with feelings and experiences that I had

known too — it seemed to read as a largely 'normal' expression of the way things are, from anyone who would like a better community.

'Why don't my friends feel like this, then?' she asked.

'They probably do, thought it might just be too raw for them to admit it. I think I felt myself that I could not have put some of my own more unhappy feelings so plainly into words.'

'Hmm, there's worse than that,' she said, sadly.

We turned to the last part of the first letter where she wrote 'It is wrong of me to want other people to help me. I am like an old woman of fifteen years old.' I couldn't help smiling at this, and looked up to see her grinning too. This presented me with an opportunity to re-enter my role as her English teacher; I reminded her of Blake's gloom-filled poem, 'The Sunflower', that we had worked on some months before in class:

> Ah, sunflower, weary of time,
> Who countest the steps to the sun,
> Seeking after that sweet golden clime
> Where the traveller's journey is done:

> Where the youth pined away with desire
> And the pale virgin shrouded in snow
> Arise from their graves, and aspire
> Where my sunflower wishes to go.

'Is that how you feel?'

Sarah: Well, I did when I wrote the article. But writing it helped. I don't feel like that now. Sometimes I'm like that.

'Do you think sunflowers *do* feel like that?'

Sarah: I don't know . . . (*grinning*)

'They don't look like that, do they?'

'Where do you think the sunflower *does* want to go?'

We recalled the earlier lesson.

'Don't you think Blake is being a bit too sad about sunflowers?'

Sarah: He probably felt really fed up, like I did . . .[3]

As I had seen a more animated side to Sarah since the publishing of the article, her second letter, which was delivered at my door a few days later during a free period when she 'should' have been in the library, came as something of a surprise. I was busy marking, but led mainly by a sense of obligation that she ought to be getting down to the work she liked best — literary studies — I dug out a passage from the beginning of Golding's *Free Fall* for her to read, while I read the letter, which dwelled in what was to become a too familiar way on her feelings and her faults:

I am unsociable. Sometimes, when my mind is no longer involved with other people I think about my faults. I seem to have a lot of faults, and it is not just because I am being over-critical. I know I am over-critical with other people and myself but at the moment I am just being honest about the way I see myself. Perhaps what I consider to be my faults, are not faults in somebody else's view but that's the way it is. I suppose some of my faults are not obvious to the people about me and probably the only way they would realize them would be by reading my work. I find it very difficult to accept changes and often, at first, I refuse to accept them. I hate changing from my surroundings and people yet eventually I do desire something else. When the change is created by myself because I feel it is necessary, it's alright but when the change takes place while I am feeling insecure, then I hate it. Although I know it is wrong, change means insecurity to me. I suppose I prefer everything to run dry before I leave it and move on. At the moment I want to change the way I am living. I want to get out of school, I want to move away from my family but if I had had to leave school a year ago I would have felt resentful. I did not want anything to change, now I do. Sometimes I think I dislike change because I am spoilt. Although there are five children in my family, I think we have all been spoilt. Perhaps I just want my own way all the time and change means I can't have this.

I find I am becoming more and more absorbed in myself, leaving very little time for other people. I feel more at peace when I am alone and when I do mix with other people I find I have a confusion inside me. It does not seem real. When I walk through the park with David, John and Nick, I do not feel as though I am me. I feel like I am acting a role and it seems strange, totally unreal. When I walk through the park by myself, like when I come home from work on Saturdays, I talk aloud to myself and I feel completely content. Probably half an hour before I was at work, worrying about something I had said to somebody, or something that had been said to me and all the feelings of tension, depression, etc., become mixed up inside me. Then I am alone in the park and nothing matters any more. People, words, emotions, they are nothing. I ridicule my thoughts and feelings because it seems impossible to take them seriously. That's the way it always is for me when I do not feel weighed down because of living.

(March, fifth year)

Along with its self-criticism about her lack of adventurousness in life, this letter could also read as a 'declaration of intent' to do something about it — to involve herself more actively in her own growth and change. Having suggested this to her, I played teacher, and asked her what she thought of the *Free Fall* passage, where the hero describes his cheerful upbringing in the squalid surroundings of a rural slum. Did she see from this that an appreciative memory of time and living past need not be exclusively sad, that the little craftsman, fixed and compulsive in his ways, was like that because he really *was* old (not an 'old woman of fifteen years . . .')? Sarah silently pointed out a sentence: 'There is a sense in which when we emerged from our small slum and were washed, the happiness and security of life was washed away also.'

'Very clean person — please don't touch,' I said; she laughed.

'How can life flow back?' I asked.

She didn't reply, then: 'Like you say sometimes, be in touch with each other. But I can't.' (*very quietly*)

'It can be misunderstood?'

Sarah: Hmmm.

It seemed she wished to be 'in touch' with others, but did not wish to risk being wrongly recognized. Yet she had been both amused and pleased about her notoriety as author of an article which resulted in the suppression of the magazine.

As the term progressed she continued to reveal slight but clear shifts in outlook and actions. She continued to be reluctant about homework, and this spread to other subjects. She began to receive criticism from other teachers, specially where the demands of external examination were concerned; when taxed about this she showed an unfamiliar obstinacy of attitude, for the first time in her career at the school. This disconcerted teachers who had previously found her amenable. In the rush of the term I did not give this very much thought, but made one or two conventional approaches to her, on the lines that I was hoping she'd be studying her A-levels soon, but that she would need some O-levels first. I assumed, using the kind of shorthand mental notes that come all too easily to hard-pressed teachers, that Sarah was probably having a delayed trip through the well-known fourth year 'doldrums', before pupils emerge duly ready and prepared to submit themselves to the fifth year examination machine. In any case she was by no means the only member of the year, or of the form, to be feeling less than whole-hearted about public exams. They had all been through the process of trial O-levels and CSEs, and it was in any case a low ebb in the year, with flu and colds reducing classes severely. I noticed that it was also about this time she changed from sitting in her usual place, on the fringe of the group of girls, and moved over to two or three of the (in class) quieter, more seriously-inclined lads. She began to send in further letters regularly, and asked to see me about what she had written; this steady stream of written self-inspection continued for about a year. It seemed futile to tell her — as I tried several times — that the energy spent on this could be better spent on straight schoolwork at this crucial time in her school career. She *could not* work, happily or otherwise, she said, and could only see a way back to work through doing this kind of writing.

It came to be understood that each piece of writing required a reply, either written or, if I had time, in the form of a personal interview (usually brief, or when I was on some routine task such as ordering materials) when her writing would help us to talk more directly about her area of concern. She clearly enjoyed writing, and it seemed that her absorption here acted as at least some alleviation of her personal miseries, even if it may not have been the means by which her eventual release came.

It was not unusual for teachers to be sought out for individual contact in the school — it is likely that I myself saw a good two-thirds of her fifth year class in this way from time to time during the year, as well as students in other classes. But the output and quality of Sarah's letters made her unusual. She also gave rise to some special concern, in that almost invariably the result of a personal meeting with a pupil was a marked increase of involvement with class and English activities; but Sarah seemed to go further and further away, which gave rise to several anxious doubts in myself from time to time, about whether I was helping her at all — or even hindering her. Just before the end of the spring term, she brooded further on her anxieties about feeling increasingly remote:

Sometimes I feel lonely, yet for the amount of time I spend by myself, it is not very often. At times I ask myself if being alone is what I really want because I never used to be like that. As I have grown older I have become more intolerant with other people so it is perhaps better for me to keep myself company. I know while I was at the grammar school I used to feel worse lonely because I stayed at home all the time and remained detached from my friends at school. Now I wonder if I have just got to grow accustomed to living with other people apart from my family, or is it just a characteristic that is in my family? My dad and Ian do not seem to want friends who are always around. I know it is probably very unsociable and sometimes I cannot help feeling guilty because of my attitude towards people. It is not that I do not want friends, it's just that I do not need them around very often. Perhaps I should not say this of all friends because there are one or even two who I would not mind at any time, but perhaps I only feel this because I do not spend much time with them. I find it difficult to understand why it is necessary for some people to go shopping, etc., with friends. I do not like having to tag along with anybody or have them tag along with me, yet all the time I am by myself, I am talking to myself. I suppose that does have some significance. I know that sometimes I talk to myself because I feel self-conscious and do not want to think about how insufficient I am feeling. About seven or eight years ago I used to pretend I had a constant companion. This invented friend was always around when I needed somebody to talk to, somebody to strengthen me, but I seem to have given up this friend for the companionship of another part of myself. There is a continual conversation going on in my head, so I do not need anybody else to keep me company most of the time. I suppose that I am just being lazy because being with other people takes more of an effort than when I am alone. I do not think people find it easy to talk to me unless they know me quite well and I certainly feel awkward talking to most people. There just does not seem to be anything I need to say, yet I often think I ought to have something to say. Sometimes I am with a person and all the time I am trying to think of something to say, then I think 'Damn it! If there is nothing worth saying, don't say anything.' Probably the uneasiness I feel is transferred to the people I am with, which only makes things more awkward, because people are obviously under a strain, even if it is not very great. It irritates me sometimes when people say I do not talk enough and I think to myself, 'What do they want me to say?' Yet with some people I can talk for ages and not feel at all uneasy. Sometimes I want to be able to talk to somebody so much that I force myself to talk to them even though I do feel taut. I suppose I only make an effort when I feel people are important to me and perhaps that is not as often as it should be. When I am with a crowd of people I feel strange, almost as though, I am not me, I feel suppressed by everything but when I am with one person I can feel it is a reality. Some people cannot be with me without talking. They seem to think there is a detachment if there are not any words linking us, but this is not true. Words are not always so important. A person can talk to me and I am not even listening, my mind is on another wavelength altogether and it is not deliberate. I just do not seem to have a lot of control over my mind now, it goes where it wants to. Probably that's part of the reason why I am so bad in lessons. Before I used to have full control of my mind but now I lose most of what is said in a lesson. I hear the words but my mind does not absorb them because it is too preoccupied with my own world. I go off into dreams and thoughts as if I should not be in this world at all. I suppose it is a form of escape from the world.

(March, fifth year)

Summer term, fifth year
The letters continued during the summer term, and I expressed concern to her parents, who urged me to keep up the contact that she had made with me; they were convinced that they had a very sensitive, rather than unstable, daughter, and their conviction here helped to reassure me. Indeed there were, after all, as many signs of strength as of weakness and regres- sion in the letters written so far. The reader was rarely made to feel that there is anyone other than a 'normal' girl writing them — if each were taken individually. The recurring fixations on her sense of depression were worrying, it is true; and there was a marked lack of humour, especially in these earlier letters, which dwelled much on depressing experiences; but it was, after all, a familiar kind of writing among this age-group. The main difference in Sarah's case was the unusual length, depth and consistency of her commentary; but there was an unusually negative aspect too, in her refusal to move beyond a seemingly obsessive self-absorption.

All the first few letters dwelled strongly on what she felt to be her grow- ing self-dislike. She found herself unsociable, that she ought to 'change the way I am living'. She felt guilty about her growing thoughts of self- assertion and independence; but also (healthily and subbornly) held to them. She disclosed with some heat, in a conversation around this time, that 'It's all right if you're a boy at this school.' What did she mean? I asked. If she didn't like the boys why did she sit with David, John and Richard sometimes?

'No, I think they're really good people. But they don't have to worry

. . . they get away with things . . . answer the teacher back (*then tearful and also smiling*) — teachers think I need an aspirin or something if I talk to them like Richard does.'

'Why, have you been trying lately?' I said.

'Not really . . .'

I reflected aloud that half the people in the school — the girls — must have her problems. She ignored this, but then said she was fed up with girls, and above all she wanted to be part of the boys' group, — they were 'easier' to be with. She thought she had been self-sufficient for so long that she could hardly remember how to talk to people, she had no 'chat'. They (the lads) often teased her about her quietness, yet she could no longer be content with her own silence, nor with the imaginary person who was part of her earlier life. She emphasized again how strongly she just wanted to be part of the group, but how difficult she found it to link her 'inside' self with them 'outside'. She asked for direct guidance here. It sounded bad, I said, but again, wasn't this everyone's problem from time to time? And was there not hope in the very nature of her distress? Wasn't it because she *has* got something inside her, capable of comradely feelings, and because there *is* something attractive out there — the company offered by the boys — that her problem came about? Was she, perhaps, *trying* too hard? Wasn't it likely to take some time before she knew her new friends well, before she was close enough for their relationship to be free of anything but the friendliest teasing? She could only expect really open friendships — without rivalry and other relationship 'games' that people play and manoeuvre in, but may not enjoy — to grow gradually.

But my sermon seemed only clumsily to miss the mark. Sarah replied 'I understand . . . but I still quiver and shake when I want to speak; and I can't say what I want to . . .'

Her next letter showed increasing self-concern over a fear of derangement. She seemed more deeply anxious about what she saw as her cowardice in the face of other people's hurts here:

In some ways I am a very selfish person, because I am so caught up with my own thoughts and feelings that I often become estranged from the people about me. I am not oblivious to them. They are in the back of my mind but I do not let them come any nearer to my conscience. I feel almost a contempt for them, even though I know it is not any fault of theirs. They are the way they are, and it is I who must be stronger to prevent myself from being hurt. Sometimes, I think, if people knew the mad things that hurt me so easily, they would laugh. Of course they would laugh, because it is so ridiculous.

But, nevertheless, I still feel wounded at their words and actions. In a way, I suppose the pain I experience is really just revolving around myself and the people who I say hurt me, are innocent of this misdemeanour. How are they to know that I feel hurt by a meaningless remark? Why should they be aware of this? When people ask me why I am upset, I know to them the reason would be totally irrational and in my mind I see this, but something inside me feels raw and inflamed. My mind and feelings are in conflict; they are so detached from each other, it seems they will never reach a compromise. Sometimes I wonder why I even allow the conflict to take place in me when no matter how sane my mind sees everything, my feelings are in their own sphere of sensitivity and logic. They seem unable to absorb anything outside this sphere, so I am compelled to feel pain, by a force I cannot cope with. When the pain first hits me, my mind struggles to inject some sanity into my feelings. 'You've got to stay strong. You've got to. Don't let the pain seize control of your life, because you'll sink. You know that, don't you? It always happens like that, so forget it.'

But even while I am thinking this, a fever is taking hold of my body, gradually dragging me down. And it is ridiculous. So mad, so very mad. Half the time people have no intention of hurting me, yet there is pain. I suppose I could tell people what they do, that hurts me, but somehow I know this would be immoral because they are not deliberately trying to hurt me, so who am I to put limits on their lives? If a person was being deliberately malicious, I think I would have some resistance but when it seems to be a pain inflicted by my own state of emotions, then I am lain bare. I become moody and sullen, restricting people with me. I cannot feel at ease while this fever is in possession of my feelings and my attitude towards the people around me is confused. I do not think I have a very sane attitude towards people because I know I do not live amongst them with the lightness I should. I hear people talking together and I think 'If that was said to me I would feel involuntarily bad.' Why? Why do I have to be so vulnerable to my feelings? I am sick of it all. I know people say I am stupid and imagine it all but how come I still feel the agitation inside me? It does not matter how ridiculous it is, the feeling is there. Sometimes I think 'if I was to tell everybody why I am moody and why I feel hurt, and they took notice, they would feel that they were living in a glass-house. Everything would be jagged and tense because people would be frightened of living spontaneously. It would not only be me with an insane attitude towards people, they would have an insane attitude towards me. I suppose the world is insane, but there are different types of insanity. I would not mind if I did not seem to be living in an insanity of my own, but that is the way it seems. I know I ought to keep the mutilation I feel inside me but I cannot, and yet I do not let it show, exactly how I feel it. I feel it as a fever, in complete possession of me, but I show it sullenly and rudely. I prefer it that way because I want to try to hide the fact I am hurt, no matter how badly I succeed. When some people hurt me I think, 'Who the hell do they think they are?' I suppose I think that with most people, but it is no compensation usually. Sometimes I even wish I could just live with a few people who are gentle and sensitive but I suppose that is just looking for an easy way out of having to be stronger. Why should not I look for an escape? When your head throbs violently and you feel hot, so hot. How do you hide this mad fever? Somehow it has got to be released from within you, onto other people if necessary. I know it is wrong to make other people suffer, just because I have been hurt, but sometimes the pain seems so unjust. Even people I feel no liking for can hurt me intensely. I do not see why I should feel the pain when I know what they think and say should be of no relevance. The other day somebody who I feel nothing for, except contempt perhaps, stung me so deeply I felt almost hatred for him. I do not think he was even intending to hurt me, but what he said, wounded me and I was plunged into anguish. It is funny really, I tried desperately to convince myself it did not matter but I could feel my emotions taking hold of me. I remained where I was, trying to keep back what I was feeling but it was no good. I had to find a retreat where I could be alone. When I returned I felt a revulsion even at the sight of him and I was tortured when I had to speak to him. Usually I do not have such a violent reaction afterwards but I felt so bad, because I knew it should not have mattered what he said. What I cannot understand is, why so many things that should not matter, do matter somewhere unknown in me. One day perhaps, I won't care, and what sort of person will I be like then? Will I be hard and rational? I suppose I need to create a shell around the most sensitive part of me so that only the really important things can penetrate it. I do not want to be insensitive but somehow I have got to protect myself. Protect myself from what? Other people, my own emotions, life? I don't know but something is causing me a pain which I want to be able to force back, before it reaches the innermost part of my being. At the moment it seems so exposed and it should not be like that. I know it should not. I know that the problem is me and not other people, because the pain I feel is not usually intended. I suppose that means I create my own pain. Only one person I have known experiences my form of hurt and it helps me when I know somebody else understands. At least there is one person who does not consider me to be completely stupid. Even as kids there was something about the way we felt which kept us together. Now, I would say we are almost worlds apart, except when it comes to feeings. Then we are almost on the same wavelength.

I can talk about something which has hurt me and it will not seem strange. We can even laugh about it, but both of us know.

(April, fifth year)

This letter ends, at least, on a more reassured note, paying tribute to her elder sister's kindness and understanding. And the letter also indicated, through her self-scolding about her irrationality, that she was thinking as hard as she possibly could about how to become stronger without becoming merely more hardened.

There is little further record of Sarah's state during that summer. She did moderately well in her examinations after all and, like the rest of the fifth year, tended to avoid the school during the summer months as much as possible. Her last letter of the term dwells again on the gap between 'her' world and the world of 'others', but this time emphasizing much more the irritating 'triviality' of that other world. And the letter ends in more familiar fifth form style, as she 'talks' her way through to an appreciative memory of fooling about in the library:

When I am feeling depressed I see people as being hard and irritating. Their faults seem to loom massive in front of me and I think, 'How can we live with life as it is, with people as we are?' Yet when the sun is warm and nourishing, people seem good and worthwhile. People have not altered but my state of mind has. Half the time when I am annoyed with somebody, it is not because they have done anything so bad, it is just me who is feeling raw. One day I will be at school and some people will drive me mad with distraction. I feel I want to tell them to shut up, to just leave me in peace and I feel so irritable. That is how I sometimes feel when I am with John, Richard and David in the library. They make a joke out of everything you say and it seems childish when they twist everything so that it sounds obscene. I get frustrated because they won't be serious and I want to be serious. Sometimes when I am by myself, completely detached from everything and everybody around me, a crowd of girls will come up and start talking to me. Their giggling and girlishness just seems to grate on the part of me which is trying to escape from the way we all seem to live. The fact is, it is not anybody who is being awkward, except me, because there are times when I do not mind these people. They are the same as before but I am not feeling so highly-strung and intolerant. The reason I am sometimes apprehensive about approaching people is because I wonder if people do not get irritated, in the same way, by me. Some days I am very giggly and childish which makes me stop and wonder if I am upsetting anybody because of this. I know I irritate some people because I do not talk much to them, but knowing this only makes me more silent. John says, 'You know your trouble, Sarah. You talk too much.' And at first I felt a bit hurt, but he says it so often now, I just ignore it. A lot of people do not seem to realize what an effort it is for me to talk to certain people. There are days when I feel confidence in myself and I can talk to anybody at school. That's how I felt on Wednesday. The sun was drawing all my strength out into the open and I felt as though the day was mine. David and John and Richard were sitting in the library and they were being mad. On another day I would not have enjoyed this type of company but this day, I laughed and was stupid with them. Throughout the day I felt as though I could fly if I had wanted to. John makes me laugh more than most people at school . . .

(May, fifth year)

Her self-consciousness and inhibitions had mercifully (if only temporarily) taken flight, and were only at the edge of her experience, morally disapproving of all the sunny laughter of the moment. In this May letter she quoted D.H. Lawrence on 'Conscience':

> Conscience
> is sun-awareness
> and our deep instinct
> not to go against the sun.

Autumn term, sixth year
Sarah came back in the sixth year to study A-level English and French, and some further O-levels. I shared the teaching of the A-level group with another teacher. She seemed remote, I thought, but probably she needed time to settle down to the new work. After several weeks had passed she sought me out once more, having done little homework, to say she resented my not teaching the class for all lessons, and also felt cheated that a Languages teacher, to whom she had grown attached, was no longer teaching their set. She heard through a briefish sermon from me on the need to accept change in life, not to cling to things that no longer exist.

But she was too troubled for this to be any kind of reassurance, as her accompanying letter revealed:

Something that I gained as a person through the warmth of the people around me has snapped and I am no longer suspended, but lying on the ground, being trampled on. I do not know if I can get up. I know I have got to, but I am not sure how. I do not feel sure of anything. Not myself or the people about me. They are new and frightening. They seem to be trying to force themselves on me and I cannot accept them. They are different and I feel unsure of them. I do not mean I distrust them, I don't find them sinister, I am just not sure. My life really settled down and now I feel in a turmoil again. The way I have reacted tells me I am not very adult, or, perhaps I am too old, refusing to accept a new way of life, refusing to accept anything different to my usual routine. In *Sons and Lovers* Mrs. Morel says to her son Arthur, 'If you don't like it, alter it, and if you can't alter it, put up with it'. This is the best attitude to have but I feel resentful. Everything seems to be right and then, suddenly, without any warning, it disintegrates.

(November, sixth year)

She wrote one or two accounts around this time about one of her lessons, which she had come to dislike greatly. It became clear that she was maintaining a passive resistance against this particular lesson, where there was a fairly rigid academic approach: though she showed that her own feelings were not motivated by meanness, and she realized, without enjoying it, that her behaviour was making the teacher 'agitated'. Her description of this lesson, offered below, shows a considerable hardening of anti-school feelings (it is not to be seen as one of the letters, since it shows signs, I think of 'polished work' rather than of self-searching; it seemed in some ways, even, to be nursing the anxieties that she has been experiencing:

Classroom

I stood outside the classroom, leaning against the wall. No point in worrying now, I thought to myself, I can't conjure up homework in two minutes. I felt rather sleepy and sluggish, I could have fallen asleep had the circumstances been more attractive, still in thirty minutes time I would be able to retire to a cosy corner in the cloakroom. Peace. I realized I had been absently chewing my fingernail and I withdrew the damp finger from my mouth. Swiftly I examined each fingernail on my right hand and after a minute's consideration, I said to myself, I am glad I don't actually bite my nails, and daftly popped my finger back into my mouth. Waiting for the teacher was beginning to play on my nerves and I felt a slight agitation growing inside me. If it was I who was late, it would be, Why are you late? Explanation please. Don't let it happen again. But when it is the teacher who is late, well, that's just unfortunate. I sighed, loudly, just to make sure everybody in the immediate surroundings knew how bored I was. There was one responsive grin, so I grinned back, after all what else was there for me to do? Five of us were left standing in the silent corridor, nobody bothered to speak, but as the teacher loomed into the distance, I was aware that I was not the only person who felt disheartened. In what seemed like no time at all, I was sitting by the radiator, fumbling with a couple of books. I heard the word 'homework' mentioned but I pretended that I had not.

'Sarah! Have you got any homework for me?' she asked with some impatience.

I shook my head, my eyes averted from the direction in which the voice had come from. I had meant to be very polite, and apologize but somehow I could not cope with words, so I remained insolently silent.

'And why not?' she asked.

What a ridiculous question, I thought to myself, and just shook my head again. However, after a quick reflection I added a shrug of the shoulders and a foolish grin. I knew it was the wrong thing to do but I felt too drowsy and bored to answer such an unnecessary question. Everybody knew I was lazy.

'Tomorrow morning, then, without fail', and with that, she turned to a pile of books on the desk, while I nodded fervently, still grinning.

I sat staring out of the window while the teacher found some work for us to do. Anything she gave us was difficult, but reading out loud, now that was something worth dreading.

'Seite drei und sechzig.'

I flicked through the thick green book. Why did she always say the number of the page in German? It always took me half of the lesson just trying to find the right page.

'Martin, will you begin reading?' the teacher asked.

I perched on the edge of my chair in order to see which page his book was open at. Just as he came to the end of his passage the number of the page became apparent and I hastily turned to the page in my book.

'Carry on, Sarah,' urged the voice from the front of the classroom.

Instantly I stiffened, like a cat which was afraid, I felt hot and clammy because I was so tense, I felt useless. Everybody was waiting for me to speak and I couldn't. My throat was so dry that I knew if I tried to speak, only a croak would come out. Silence. I could have cried but that would have been of no avail. I placed my finger on the first word I was to read and I began. Slowly and toneless. Every time I pronounced a word wrong, the teacher corrected me and I had to repeat it. The more this happened the worse I felt. My fingers clutched at my cardigan, searching for something firm and my hair flopped over my eyes so that I kept losing the line I was reading from. I had read half of my passage and then, a blockage set itself in my mind. I just couldn't read any more, everything had been squeezed out of me. I sat, staring at the page.'Can't she see I can't read anymore,' I thought to myself. 'Why doesn't she choose somebody else and leave me alone?' I bit my lip, and frowned heavily. I felt deeply resentful. Why do I have to go through this ordeal every time? I was on the verge of walking out or just crying when she said: 'Will you finish reading Paul?'

I did not sigh inside me or feel relieved. I carried on staring at the words, they were dead. I did not dare look up or show any signs of consciousness, because while I seemed dead nothing would be expected of me.

As the lesson came to an end I began to unwind. Very slowly and with uncertainty. I was the first to leave the room. Out of the clutches of tension and distress I felt like a wet rag.

More productively, she was reading Lawrence's *The Rainbow,* a book of her own choice, which, she declared, she was enjoying more than our set A-level texts. No *French Lieutenant's Woman* for her, I thought, but one must work with the grain. I drew her attention to the passage where Ursula is asked by her father to help with the potato-planting; here, Lawrence evokes the gap between the child's and the adult's view, corresponding in part, perhaps, to Sarah's sense of 'inside' and 'outside' reality. I wanted to suggest that her suffering did not make her odd, that her plight was familiar (as I believe it is, though rarely so clearly articulated). Ursula is a small child, of whom little could be expected in terms of self-help. For Sarah, I suggested, I felt all the sympathy that was easy to give to Ursula, in her smallness and infant vulnerability; but wasn't she (Sarah) in a much more potentially powerful position than that of a helpless child? Couldn't she take some effective steps *herself* towards bridges being built, contacts being made?

A few days later she handed in, in her own handwriting, a short passage from later in the book, when Ursula is near to Sarah's own age, feeling gloom at the prospects ahead:

> . . . As Ursula passed from girlhood towards womanhood, gradually the cloud of self-responsibility gathered upon her. She became aware of herself, that she was a separate entity in the midst of an unseparated obscurity, that she must go somewhere, she must become something. And she was afraid, troubled. Why, oh why must one grow up, why must one inherit this heavy, numbing responsibility of living an undiscovered life? Out of nothingness and the undifferentiated mass, to make something of herself! But what? In the obscurity and pathlessness to take a direction! But whither? How take even one step? And yet, how stand still! This was torment indeed to inherit the responsibilty of one's own life.

> D.H. Lawrence, *The Rainbow,* Chapter XI

The few brief meetings that we had from then until Christmas took a happier form of teacher-learner talk on *The Rainbow,* especially the late part of the book which involved Ursula's growing into womanhood.

Spring term, sixth year

Sarah had still not returned to anything like what was known as a 'good sixth-form attitude', and this Spring term brought about a crisis for her. Again she wrestled with contrary feelings about her need for warmth and intimacy of fellowship, but also her need to be alone. Yet despite her opening confession of feeling 'stale', she takes the debate further and deeper in her next letter:

> I feel stale. The staleness grows gradually, so nobody is aware of it, then it hits you, deep inside and you are not really sure what to do about it. I feel I want to shut my eyes and let everything drift away so that I will wake into a fresh and new world. The shrivelling up of my inner self must stop before I become an empty vessel, because I cannot live like that. I need to be myself, not what other people need me to be.
>
> People around this place do not seem to be as important to me as they were once, and I wonder why this should be. I have become closer to people in this school yet I also feel as though I have drifted a long way from them. This time last year I was more detached from my class than I am now and I did not mind being that way. At the time I needed the solitude and calmness

of my own company. Other people were very casual in their acquaintance with me so I did not know anybody very well, and I think that could be the reason I feel so far away from people. When you only have a shallow contact with people, things do not seem important really. You do not know what deep and complex feelings they have and you are not bothered much about being in touch with them. You do not really know the people as they are when they are themselves, so you do not have anything to understand. They just seem a bit superficial and you cannot care that neither of you understand each other because there is nothing real between you. You do not know what is important in their life so there is no way of being sure of how far or near you could be to them. They are just people who, as far as you can see, are alright to have around. Everything is just easy-going. Then you get to know people and a loneliness creeps in. Perhaps other people do not feel in this way but I do. Even though some of the people I know are very real I still feel a desire to stay within myself because I cannot help being aware of my actual aloneness. No matter how much I am involved with other people I will always be alone, and the more I know people, the clearer this solitude becomes. I know these people better than I have ever known them and yet I now see how far away I am as an individual. It is very difficult to explain what I mean. I do not feel in touch with people even though they are always with me, talking to me. Somehow I feel on a different wave-length to people I associate with. Perhaps everybody is on their own wave-length, I do not know. It seems so confusing because I cannot put into words exactly what I feel.

Quite often while I am at school I feel very frustrated because I cannot get away from people. I am alone in myself, in the deepest part of me but sometimes I want to be completely alone. They are everywhere, talking. Talking to me, at me and it just blurs my mind. I get so bored and irritated that it does not do other people nor myself any good. I am getting very hung up about this and if it continues I am going to become even more edgy and intolerant. I suppose it is pointless me writing about bossy teachers because most people are aware of the tension they cause by their pettiness. I just want them to leave me alone. Once I could laugh them off but after a couple of years they seem to have become too much for me. I think my general attitude towards everything at the moment makes me more irritated by this school and its dictators, but they are still there, trying to force me into the mechanical routine of the school. Why cannot I sit in the cloakroom instead of the common room at dinner-time? I am not a person who enjoys the atmosphere of the common-room so why am I supposed to rush there and join in? I saw a play a short while ago where a boy did not like the roughness of the boys in his school. He did not get any pleasure from the Christmas parties his headmaster arranged. In fact he seemed to hate them with an immense fear. When the boy asked to be excused from the party the headmaster was astonished. He had the idea firmly fixed in his head, that boys love Christmas parties. They should enjoy parties and have a good time, so the boy had to go to the party. How can the headmaster or anybody decide what the boy does and does not enjoy? Why should a teacher decide for me where I am to spend my time?

Probably our school is too large for everybody to be where they want to be, I do not know. One morning I had been in this school just ten minutes and I was moaned at by three teachers for being in the wrong place at the wrong time. I was not making a noise. I was not trying my utmost to destroy the loos. I was just reading alone. Some teachers seem to be rather insincere at times. They do not shout or order me around as M.B. does. They are very polite, as if they are just asking me to do something, when I know very well they expect me to do it, no matter how I feel. They smile friendly as if to cover up the fact that they have just given me an order. I will shut up moaning about the teachers in this school because it does not do any good and the more I think about it, the more bitter I feel. Probably if I did not feel so depressed and bored I would see the real goodness there is in some of the teachers.

I feel I need to get away from this place and the people in it because things can only get worse. Probably I am the only person who can twist everything round so that I do know where I am going, yet I do not have the energy. I have got a strange desire to be like a waterfall but I am not alive and fresh enough. I just feel so stale and tired. I want to feel real enthusiasm for something, but there does not seem to be anything. I suppose I have got to search for something, I just do not know. My mind seems to be clogging up so that it is now difficult to really think about anything. Sometimes I feel so lazy and bored I accept what I am told, without a moment's reflection. I am frightened I could be dying as an individual person, with my own life . . .

(January, sixth year)

After reading this, I decided to ask Jim, my co-teacher of the A-level sixth to have a word with her too. He proved to be helpful, in sharing the time that Sarah demanded, and especially in his unsentimental, apparently carefree approach. Jim and I agreed that we would back up what her own friends seemed to be doing for her, as far as possible, by appealing especially to her sense of humour. But we would still show her that we accepted what she had to say, lest she felt that we were trying to 'trivialize' her, or 'normalize' her, as she frequently claimed happened to people of her age. I took up her 'strange desire to be a waterfall' — a rather lovely phrase which lifts the writing about the familiar complaint of staleness and lassitude — and suggested that once again she had been able to see for herself a way out: should she not pursue that 'strange desire' in her own way? She said nothing herself, and I left her with a written comment I'd noted down on her letter, in the form of a poem by a nine-years' old Yorkshire boy (it had appeared in the *Use of English* journal):

> *The Lonely Flower*
>
> What art tha doin' there, mun
> All on thee own
> Nowt to eat and nowt to sup
> Tha looks badly thee
> Lift up they 'ead and shout for't sun
> If tha don't shake theeself
> They'll call thee Weepy Willy.

And (for good measure) I gave her a copy of Henry Vaughan's poem, 'Waterfall'. She said later that she liked this but she did not attempt to discuss or write on it, as I had hoped she might.

Her next letter showed little development of her feelings and thoughts, apart from some resentment at our too explicit encouragement that she should be more flexible and humorous. She began by almost parodying 'Weepy Willy': 'I feel a bit shivery because there is a chilly draught from the cold corridor, and I am hungry . . .' She then dwelled on the impossibility of the detachment she sought:

There seem to be so many things at the moment that are cutting me off from some people, and I am not sure I want to be like that. Somebody said 'opting out' of the system is cowardly and pretending everything is all right, but I do not think this is really true. How many people can actually 'opt out' altogether? I am told by some teachers that I have 'opted out' of the system of this school. But I have not. How can I have 'opted out' when I still feel pressurized by the rules and people here? I do not do what I want to do here. I rarely go to tutor groups or assembly, but what significance does that really have? Even if I do not take orders from certain people here, there are others that do, and I am here, seeing it happen. When people try to 'opt out' of a system they are still very aware of what is happening within the system. It is in full view for them as they stand looking on, and it is sickening sometimes. Most of the time actually. If I had completely 'opted out' of this school's system, I would not even be here. I keep thinking to myself, 'laugh, you must laugh,' but I do not, so I become depressed and everything seems useless, so totally useless. Every little thing that is not quite right upsets me and in the end it all builds up into a great wall surrounding me. It is dark and dank. I feel as though I am going to rot away in this morbid seclusion. Yet I always come out of the depression, just long enough to feed on the warmth and life that exists outside this prison. Up and down, up and down, so fast. Everything seems to move so fast. Everything seems to move so fast, I cannot keep up . . .

She presses further the charge of humourlessness against herself, and moves on to reveal a further complication — of 'jealousy', which is developed in subsequent letters (later, it became clear that this had very specific cause, through her having fallen in love with Richard around this time):

I do not want to have to bear the feelings I have now, knowing that they are rather ridiculous and that eventually I won't feel like that at all. I just cannot seem to accept everything the way it is, I cannot laugh my way through life which is something I regret. By taking everything so seriously am I really being myself? And if I am, I cannot do much to change can I? I do not see how I can take everything as a joke when inside I do not really feel that. Sometimes I find myself pretending I do not care, laughing away, when inside I feel so horrid I do not want to laugh or do anything. I think probably people do conceal their real feelings so much that they just eat away inside, destroying their own being, especially when the feeling is destructive in itself . . . My moods change so unreasonably fast, I just do not seem to remain stable for any great length of time. I suppose I ought to make sure I do not let my emotions get out of hand, because then everything does seem impossible. People say, 'Keep everything in perspective', and I know I do not always do this, so perhaps that explains the confusion I get in . . . I suppose I ought to just realize how I am feeling and accept it, but how can I accept such destructive feelings as jealousy? Part of me says, 'You do not let the jealousy out, so you do not really hurt anybody,' but something deep inside me says, 'No, I do not let it out. I do not hurt people with it, but it's destroying me. It's eating away inside me and it's making me feel bad.' Perhaps I am being selfish now, but it is a sickening feeling when it keeps recurring.

(February, sixth year)

A further (long and extremely miserable) letter followed close on this one, where she wrote relentlessly on her growing confusion about these new 'possessive' and 'jealous' feelings, which seemed at the time (for she had not admitted her love for Richard) to stem from her merely envying her friends for their apparent freedom from pain and confusion:

I feel so unused to people that everything they say catches onto me and strangles me. I feel that I am just struggling, struggling, trying to free myself from the people around me; because I cannot cope. I honestly feel I cannot cope. Sometimes I think, why is not there just one person who feels the same as me? Because I am tired of trying to explain to people how I feel when really they blindly nod in agreement because they are just not interested. They do not care about my confusion but I suppose I cannot blame them, it is so deep inside me I do not think it will ever leave me, it's embedded within me because I am not strong enough to uproot everything. I want to be the real me but when I am people seem to think I am strange and then I feel an outcast. I do not feel many people accept me, but sometimes I think I do not accept myself either. I watch people as they talk and fool around in their own crowds and I wonder why I cannot enjoy that way of being. At school and at work on Saturdays, I feel I am just not part. At work I sit at the back of the room by the window and radiator and that seems to be just about it. The other seven girls chat about pop stars, boyfriends and pubs and I am completely out of touch with them. I seem to sit in my corner looking out of the window and although I prefer this to talking to the rest of the girls, somehow I feel I ought to enjoy talking about these sort of things. Whenever I get around to talking to people I want to start talking about something serious and not really what those people want to talk about. I have to know how people really feel because if I do not I just do not feel sure of them. Sometimes I find people feel and think very differently to what it seems . . . I wish that people would talk more about how they really feel, instead of covering up and fooling around. I do not mean telling the truth all the time because that can be hurtful, I just want to be able to know where I stand with people . . . I find people confusing because sometimes I want them to be considerate and gentle and they are not. The more I dwell on the thought the more thoughtless people seem to be. When I walk along a street, seeing everybody rushing about I feel, almost, a dislike for human beings in general and it depresses me because I know there is much goodness in people . , . To some people I will explain my feelings and emotions. I can say to them, sometimes I feel very possessive and jealous and they will believe me. They will not laugh at me nor despise me. They will understand. Some people probably would not imagine me feeling jealous or even cruel.

(February, sixth year)

The next letter was calmer, and written after a short illness. She tells of her disappointment that our school seems to have become so pressing for examination standards, so like the old grammar school she knew, instead of offering the release she had naïvely hoped for. Then, deflated, she wonders whether after all it is not she who is 'bad', rather than the school system. The letter then dwells especially on her lack of boy-friend experience, and how hard she is trying to put this right by seeking to understand people more. She describes how she has been keeping a diary for some time (on top of the long letters), purely to record her day-to-day responses to people:

I am sitting in bed, one minute feeling very depressed and the next minute feeling as though I am really going to live. I have been thinking about when I first came to this school because something which had seemed so full of hope and freshness has disintegrated around me. Perhaps it seems like an exaggeration to most people but that is how I feel. When I first came here I felt frightened because I felt it was a fault in myself that made me dislike my other school. I came here with one thought in my mind: 'If I do not like this school, then there is definitely something wrong in me. The schools are not bad, it is just me.'

The years I spent in the Grammar School were bad for me in several ways but one thing (some people may consider it trivial) which has caused me a lot of confusion is the fact that it was an all-girls' school. If I had been a different sort of person I would not have been affected in the way I was but I was introvert and lacked confidence. Try to imagine living from the age of 11½ to 14 without speaking to a boy of that age or having any contact with the opposite sex. Probably people will think: 'What do a couple of years matter?' But you see, they matter a great deal, especially at that age when you are developing as a complete individual. If I had made friends out of school perhaps I would not have found things so difficult but I was too shy to go out anywhere, so I stayed indoors, shut away from the realities of life. By not growing up with boys of my age I did not have a chance to understand them. When I was thirteen I still thought of boys as having the same

mentality as the boys I knew in my junior school. I came to a stand-still during
those years, so when I came here I was completely lost. I had forgotten how
to live with boys my own age and how to be friends with them. There was
no spontaneity. I am just writing about how I was affected because I know
that probably only a few are affected as I was.

Before we moved house and I went to the Grammar School, I used to be
friends with the boy next door, who was a couple of years older than me.
We had been friends for years and while I was at the Grammar School I never
saw him, but he was the only boy I could remember ever really knowing and
I fretted over him. I suppose people would laugh because of my age but, you
see, if I had been at a mixed school I would have hardly thought of him the
way I did. When something is missing, it suddenly becomes ridiculously important. There were no boys and it was very unnatural so I had to fill the
gap with the only boy who had meant anything to me. Also I knew I would
not feel at ease with a boy but I could remember feeling completely at ease
with him. He was a scapegoat. Somehow it all seemed unhealthy. It seems
so stupid to be cut off from boys like that when you have eventually got to
live in a mixed community and possibly marry one. How can you be expected
to leave school at eighteen years old and mix naturally, when you have hardly
spoken to a boy? How can you cope with emotional problems when you have
never had a chance to experience anything on a lighter level? I know this
sounds exaggerated and drastic but honestly emotional problems are not all
that easy to cope with. Once again I am speaking for myself because I know
a lot of people would not get so muddled and confused as me. Being inhibited
is a terrible drawback in life . . . I am the sort of person who needs things
to be gradual and sure.

I am not really sure why I am writing all this. I suppose I just need to look
back on how I have developed and grown up. Really I should not use the
term 'grown up' because I have not grown up. Sometimes my emotions run
riot with me and then I realize I am not mature enough to cope with my feelings. I have tried but I honestly do not know what to do. I cannot eliminate
feelings that are in me, even if I do not want them. I have kept a diary for
a long time but for the last four months I have kept an exercise book in which
I have recorded my attitudes towards people. I have not written in it every
day, just when I have needed to write, and as I read through it now I notice
how my feelings about certain people have developed. It has helped me tremen-
dously, because, even though on some days it is obvious I have misundestood
somebody, I can tell by what I write on a later date, that I have sorted it all
out. I do not try to deliberately connect each piece I write. They are independent, yet time and again I find I have either contradicted myself, or

strengthened a point I made earlier. I know people think I am secretive but I just prefer to take my time before I really commit myself. By writing exactly how I feel, I can try to understand myself. Perhaps I sound conceited but I know I am very honest with myself. I cannot pretend to have feelings when I have not. Sometimes I have tried to pretend to feel the opposite to how I do actually feel, but it is useless. Automatically a hidden person in me laughs and says, 'Come off it. You know you do care. Don't try to fool me.' Then I laugh, because it seems so funny to have two people inside me, having such a good-humoured disagreement. The honest person in me always wins which can be painful sometimes.

Writing has helped me a lot because when I was at the grammar school I never used to discuss my feelings or thoughts with anybody, and neither did I write them, so everything got bottled up inside me. The only way I expressed any of my mixed-up feelings was by crying. I always cried, just so that I did not become so full of unexpressed feelings that I exploded.

I think the reason I cannot talk to a lot of people is because I have not got much of a social self. Most people seem to have a social self and a private self, but I seem to be rather lacking in the first. Some people tend to consist mainly of a social self with a very small private self, and this is not particularly satisfactory either . . .

Her self-analysis here becomes definitive, I think. She talks about her lack of 'social self', a lack which results in her feeling much too exposed to others. She has mentioned this before, but never so clearly. She expresses great concern here about the choice of roles to be made, and the letter concludes by stating a very clear rejection of the role that she feels has been allotted to her by other people — industrious student passes exams and becomes teacher. Yet she fears too for the future, feeling that 'there is nothing real ahead of me':

I do not think I accept myself as I am, yet how can I ever expect to be happy when I am dissatisfied so often? I am dissatisfied with this school, so I intend leaving, but I know, as well as everybody else, that this is no solution, because there is nothing real ahead of me. I feel sure a lot of people think I have wasted any intelligence I have, and I can see how they feel, but I am growing up, and I have got to be the one to decide what I do. I am not mature and I will make mistakes but I know if I stay on at school and sit more examinations I will become resentful, blaming other people for the position I am in. People say to me, 'One more year is not long. It will fly by. Do your A-levels, then you can do what you want.' I really can understand what they mean, because

I have told myself this so many times but the thought of sitting hours doing exams frightens me so much I feel physically weak and sick. I can see I should try to work hard so that I can get A-levels but the enthusiasm just is not in me so it would be completely useless. Also, I feel very restricted here. Somehow I need to get out of the routine because I have been here too long.

(February, sixth year)

When she came back to school she sought me out, and seemed calmer in herself, though still pale with illness. There was a flu epidemic in the school, with many classrooms little more than half-full, and I showed her a poem I had been hawking round my classes:

Being visited by a friend during illness

I have been ill so long that I do not count the days;
At the southern window, evening — and again, evening.
Sadly chirping in the grasses under my eaves
The winter sparrows morning and evening sing.

By an effort I rise and lean heavily on the bed;
Tottering I step towards the door of the courtyard.
By chance I meet a friend who is coming to see me;
Just as if I had gone specially to meet him.
They took my couch and placed it in the setting sun;
They spread my rug and I leaned on the balcony-pillar.
Tranquil talk was better than any medicine;
Gradually the feelings came back into my numbed heart.

Po Chü-i, trans. Arthur Waley

The cue for that short interview came from the last lines — a quiet walk together through the school playground just before the lunch-time rush, watching a squirrel playing and running along the wooden fence of the ground, to dart away invisibly at the end.

Her next letter seemed a great step forward, where she writes directly of her attachment to Richard:

I feel much straighter now than I have for quite a while but still one thing is troubling me. I have never mentioned about Richard before because I kept thinking I could stop myself feeling as I did. Everytime I was going to talk about it, part of me said, 'Perhaps the feeling will go soon,' and I kept silent. I know it sounds very silly, but it has hurt me a lot. I do not want to continue crumpling under the force of people but sometimes I cannot sustain myself. I suppose that is why eventually I have to talk to somebody about what is worrying me. I need them to strengthen me even though I know I should be able to support myself. Everything is just so hard sometimes, I feel I cannot stand it any more, but eventually I do rise and try to face it, yet I get knocked down again. I get up, and fall down again, and again, and again. Sometimes I wonder why I do get up when I can predict what will happen. I suppose it is just something that is in human beings. No matter how hard everything seems, there is some hope. It's this hope that makes people keep trying, but surely the hope must wear out. Exhausted by the terrible torture that has been inflicted. I mean, this hope, it cannot last forever, can it? Surely the time will come when you feel, that's it, I cannot get up and fight any more. It's over and I am just going to sink deeper into defeat. It's strange, only part of me has hope, the rest of me knows the uselessness of it all. It knows what will eventually happen, but this small part of me tries and tries, just hoping. Hoping. Why does that part of me refuse to accept the obvious? I suppose it would be almost impossible to live without hope. Forever hoping, hoping things will change, hoping things will improve, but how often do they? Although I seem depressed a lot, I have still got hope in me. I do not think I would be even as strong as I am now if it was not for that. People hope that their wages will rise, hope life will be more free, hope for this, hope for that. We would be almost dead if we did not hope, no matter how useless. The worst thing is when the hope is continually beaten down. It gets more and more difficult to retrieve the pieces and build yourself up again. Harder, and harder, until at last, it's the end. You do not get up any more. It is sordid and depressing. It is rather like disintegrating, but it does take so much strength to keep coming back with the renewed hope and belief in everything. I suppose there are some people who always seem to come back, fighting with the same vitality and strength.

Perhaps my form of hope at the moment is trivial but I do not really know how I can say this when I know what I have felt and what I feel now. It is strange how people, and myself even, laugh and say, 'You'll get over it. It is not so important,' when no matter how unreal it will seem in the future, now it is so very real.

I do not want to let myself be dominated by Richard and although I know

I am probably going to look back on this and laugh, it hurts now. That's the worst of it. Everything is really so ridiculous I ought to be laughing my head off, but I am not. Sometimes when I am going home from school, I walk along the street muttering to myself and laughing ironically at the different feelings I have had during the day, but it does not stop the nagging pain inside. Even the fact that most young people feel the same, some time or other, does not help much. In a way it is a lonely feeling and you cannot imagine anybody feeling as bad as you do. It's you and nobody else. I personally find it very difficult to discuss, and even more so, to write. Usually when something is worrying me I can write easily about it, but this is an effort. Perhaps I should not try to write about it, if it is so difficult but I feel almost as though I have had enough of it all. I just want to empty it all out of me. I know a year is too long for this to drag on, but I could not seem to stop the way I felt, of my own accord, and even now, that seems useless. I personally do not think I am creating a complete image of him for myself. Since I last spoke to you I have tried to keep sane but I do not feel a bit successful. If I can keep my mind occupied I do not feel so bad but sometimes my mind has wandered without me realizing it. This is not the first time I have tried to get over it and I wonder why I am so weak in my attitude.

(March, sixth year)

Really she seemed hardly ready to cope with the strength of relationship that she wanted with him (and how about *his* readiness for *her*?). But she records how she has found a new strength in herself — wobbly and unreliable, as yet — but she believes in it, and it is not, she declares, just a dependence on, or losing herself in, Richard. She is aware of the danger of 'creating a complete image of him for myself' and decides that she has not in fact done this (one thing that seems clear about Sarah is that she was not self-deceiving, but was remorselessly honest about her fears and fantasies). There is a tentative 'return to laughter' towards the end of the letter, but only in part. The letter ends with a further plea for help. I took the line with her that there seemed to be many signs of hope in this letter — whether things went well with Richard or not.

The next letter seemed at first to be a relapse; the solution to her problem seemed to be nowhere in sight:.

At the moment I am writing because I feel jealous and emotionally upset. My face feels hot and I want to cry but I will not let myself. Not now, I cannot. You build up your own illusions and then suddenly they are shattered . . .

Yet a new feeling emerges, a constructive anger with herself, prompted clearly by a quarrel with Richard:

I ought to live without other people's help, especially now . . . Do not I write a lot of boring rubbish? If I had not written this I think I would feel so terribly depressed. I do not know why I have to be like this. It is all so ridiculous. I keep saying that but it makes no difference whatsoever. I think I ought to decide about something important. Not just writing this sort of rambling rubbish, because it has not got any definite meaning. Well, nothing that would interest anybody except me. It does not interest me that much, but it is something to do. Something to keep my mind so full that there is no room for anything important. It is funny how sometimes I try so hard to prevent myself from thinking about something. Don't think! Don't think! I keep saying this but it does not really work, because it is still there, worrying and worrying. Eating away. Destroying. I would not have thought one person would feel so much destruction in them.
The sun is shining into the library, everything should be fresh and wonderful, but it is not. Not in me. When I feel like this I know I have got to go away. Of course it is running away, but I am sick of the misery I am creating for myself by staying here. I am almost condemning myself to depression and misery by my attitude. I know I create most of it for myself, but not all of it. Honestly I do not. I must not dwell on what is upsetting me. Shut myself off from it. Some people would probably think this a bad idea but it is not really. If I never shut my mind off, I will eventually get so twisted I will go mad. Don't you think so? I do not even know who I am talking to, so perhaps I am mad. Have you ever considered that? I always used to think that when people were mad they did not know it. I seem to be going round and round. Very depressing. Never reaching a straightforward decision. I do not know why on earth I cannot think a bit straight for once, or be able to reach a sensible decision without taking such a long time and without getting depressed in in the meantime. I cannot stand the illogical way I think at the moment. I am so irrational and stupid, it is incredible. I suppose I am not the only person like it, am I? I would like to meet somebody who is as ridiculous in their way of thinking and feeling as me. There must be somebody, but where? I think I'll talk to Mr A. but perhaps he does not want me bothering

him today. He can tell me to go away if he really wants to. Nobody has to put up with me if they do not want to . . . I am not logical, I do not think logically as some people do. Perhaps they just seem to, and underneath they are in just as much a muddle as me . . .

(March, sixth year)

She is tempted to find someone else to talk to but is also reluctant, for a new voice is struggling against regression to former states of depressed dependence. She says that (a) writing helps *and* (b) 'it's a lot of boring rubbish'. The passage develops with a certain vein of sharp irony against her 'old' self. She relapses somewhat when contrasting her state with the sun's 'shining into the library'; but then she restores the self-mocking ironic tone towards the end. She is aware of a new distinction in herself, between the vulnerable 'artist' self and the more strongly emerging sensible, rational Sarah who scolds that dependant, pining, but sharply honest inner voice (one thinks of Lear and the Fool, where the Fool has become the dominant character, and Lear tries manfully to re-establish some *outside* authority *in the world,* for himself). She seems to want to provoke her reader in this letter — 'I do not know who I am talking to, so perhaps I am mad. Have you ever considered that?' And, 'nobody is going to read it, so what can it matter?' followed by an attack on 'sensible people' who are probably 'in just as much muddle as me'. This I took to be a criticism of my 'non-intervention' approach at that time. It also showed a welcome self-assertion — that she did not need us anyway, in her day-to-day battle to stand up for herself.

The last few letters seemed to confirm this turning-point, and there was virtually no discussion rising from them. She was clearly enjoying the company of her small group much more, and was more secure with Richard. Her writing from now on was much more a recording of *good* times:

I feel disgusted with myself for being the person I have been recently. This time I have really frightened myself because I have just realized the type of person I could always be if I allow myself to remain in this rut . . . Richard, John and David are about the only people who can make me laugh wholeheartedly at myself and that makes me feel better. When I tell my mum about them she thinks I have got a crush on them but she does not know me very well now. I have not got a crush on them, I just feel a strong affection for them, which is love, but a certain type of love. They make me feel as though

I am smiling inside when we walk through Rosehill Park and they start to have a grass fight, I stand and watch them running about, grass flying everywhere, and I laugh and laugh, everything seems so good and happy. What I feel for them is somewhere deep inside and I cannot explain properly. Sometimes I feel I want to hug them and tell how much they matter to me, but it's just something inside; so I only laugh at their madness. I feel something for Richard but it's a different feeling. Perhaps it's a crush, my mum would think so if I tried to explain why I do not work at school, why I'm moody, etc. I have never felt like this before but the feeling has been in me well over a year so what do I do? I do not know what to do and I realize how much of a child I am. I have wanted him to ask me out all this time but I never forced my company on him because I did not seem to have the right. In some ways I think I'm very prudish, I cannot stand boys kissing me or anything unless I feel a lot for them. As much as I feel for Richard anyway. This probably seems very stupid but that's the way I am. When Richard started kissing me over the park, I suddenly thought, 'I must stop now because to him I could be any girl, while to me, he's him, nobody else.' Afterwards I thought about it and decided I could be wrong so I let it go on. But what's the good of a relationship between 9 a.m. and 3.30 p.m? Part of the reason I do not do any work is because the only time I see him is at school. All right, so I'm letting myself be carried away by my feelings. I admit that, and I'm totally mixed-up because of it. On Friday he told me he was coming to the barbecue with a girl. He said he was not actually going out with her, his friend had just stopped going out with her and so he was looking after her until she got over it. He asked me if I minded and at first I said what I thought I should feel. 'No I do not mind. I'm not going out with you so it does not matter.' He said, 'That's how it should be,' and I felt horrid. Not really through jealousy this time. I was a bit jealous but it was more because I suddenly felt that all along he had just been playing around and I had not, so I said 'No, it should not be like that.' I honestly did not mean to put him in that situation, I did not want to let out by bitchiness or anything. I wanted to be sensible but when tears and pain come, I cannot seem to stop them. I think that when I feel hurt I become hard and cold. I should never have got a seventeen year old boy in such a confusion because of how I felt. I cannot cope with my feelings so I should have been more careful with him. What I meant to say would not come out and I always get mixed-up when I'm upset. I said one of the most selfish and horrid things I could have said to him. I said, 'You don't care a damn about me.' I did not really mean it in that sense because why should he care? I meant, 'Why did not he say he just wanted to have a laugh?' I am over-demanding are not I? I seem to possess all the feelings

I despise, like possessiveness and jealousy and look what I have expected of Richard?

If you can talk to me, I'd be grateful. You can shout at me if you like but tell me something at least.

(March, sixth year)

Here she confesses to guilt feelings at having *admitted* her aggressions, then reflects sensitively, on behalf of them both, on the problems brought about by her growing love for Richard, wondering about the weight of her demands on him.

This was followed by a delightful letter, where she recorded her growing confidence and sense of freshness, looking back on her past miseries, and paying tribute to Jim, my colleague:

'I have found the last few months very difficult, and many times I have just wanted to hide away from everything. To crawl into a shell and protect myself from the madness which seemed to surround me. In fact the madness was in me, not around me. Instead of taking a sane look at the way I was feeling I think I must have let myself get caught up in it, because I do not see how I could have got so confused and depressed otherwise. I am not sure why talking to Mr. A. made me see most people did accept me, but it did. Perhaps the sun with its warmth and energy is awakening a freshness in me, because I really do feel better. I am growing up and it is so hard, I almost feel a hatred for it, but I think I am probably accepting things better. Myself especially. When I think about the past few months I see I must have developed a rather unhealthy attitude towards people, and, instead of laughing at it, I took it seriously, allowing it the one source of nourishment it needed to grow and grow. Entwining itself round my mind. That was a bad thing for me to do because my mind became imprisoned and any fresh thoughts were forbidden to take root. My mind was unable to search for the sanity it needed in order to heal the pain I had inflicted on myself.

While I was talking to Mr. A. the other day he said, 'In some ways people are very generous,' and at last something was able to penetrate the growth enclosing my thoughts. For the first time in a long while I looked at the people around me with a different attitude. I did not think straight away, 'Yes, people are extraordinarily understanding and kind.' I was very careful. For months I had been dominated by the same thoughts and I was not going to change that abruptly, but something in me felt much lighter when people talked to me. I did not feel slow and sluggish as if I could not be bothered with anybody or anything. I wanted to talk to people who in the past I had made no effort to be sociable with. I had been under the impression the people regarded me with distrust but now I was aware that they either saw me as I was, or just did not see me. Both these were better than my former feeling about it. I think the distrust must have just been in me, part of my self-inflicted prison.

'In this society people have got to be two-faced if they do not want to be shattered.' When Mr. A. first said this in our English lesson, I did not believe it. I thought: How can you trust anybody if they are two-faced? But I went out of the lesson, and I thought and thought because as Mr. A. said it, I knew it was worth considering. I thought about friends who I particularly admired and I realized that the deeper, more sensitive part of them was rarely shown to the public. I knew there was more to them, than just the sociable person they acted the role of, and this made me see why I seemed to be continually breaking up. I was exposing my deepest thoughts and feelings to people who it was not necessary to show. I did not need to open myself to everybody, on my social life. I thought, 'Sarah, you have been a fool,' but knowing me I will continue to be a fool one way or another.

(March, sixth year)

I was not wholly sure about the comments that Jim had made about the need to be 'two-faced', but Sarah seemed to have adapted the advice for herself: 'I realized the deeper, more sensitive part of them was rarely shown to the public . . .' Yet she discloses too that she is likely to remain a 'fool' — vulnerable, through her own artistic quickness and vision; a poet-fool, someone who must, from inner need, reveal eventually the truth of what she feels.

Summer term, sixth year
The next letter was really a signing-off this time, a tribute to the friendship and good work of Richard and David, especially:

I feel stronger now than I have ever felt in the last six years. Perhaps I appear a weak person to a lot of people, but I know that I am not so weak. I admit

I am rather soft and easily hurt but other people cannot sway me when I really believe something. I think I have become stronger because I feel more confident in myself and I think David and Richard have helped me a lot. People have often avoided laughing at me openly, for fear of hurting me, and although at the time I was grateful, I now realize it hindered me because I always took myself and other people seriously. I could never laugh at myself because I felt so self-conscious and inhibited that I could not bear any form of criticism, even if it was only a joke . . . David and Richard have helped me to learn how to laugh at myself because of their warmth and perseverance. When Richard first made jokes about me I felt ever so hurt and confused because I had never been really made fun of before. I used to walk into the classroom and he would call me 'Muscles', making me want to shrivel up to nothing. At the beginning I lost quite a lot of self-confidence and became more inhibited because I felt he must despise me. I really began to feel I must be weird for him to say such mad things. I do not recall feeling so hurt because of David and I think I probably felt at ease with David from the beginning. It is only very recently that I have felt able to talk to Richard, because somehow people who appear very confident in themselves make me feel uncertain of myself. I used to think I would never feel at ease with Richard but now I can talk to him and I feel grateful to him because I made no effort whatsoever to offer any friendship or warmth. It was not because I did not want to, I just could not, but Richard and David really broke through my shell and I am glad they did . . .

(April, sixth year)

A few weeks later she wrote a longish account of her primary school days — written in sharp contrast to her opening account of the grammar school. This final letter dwelled on the rebellious, 'classroom fool' — not poet fool — side of her nature. She was once again in touch with those preciously earthy, earlier memories, and was able through them to offer a more balanced view of her recent experiences:

In my junior school I used to really laugh and have a mad time during the music lessons. I can remember sitting on the low, wooden benches with my friends, playing our triangles, and tears running down our faces. Now this may seem ridiculously pointless, but it made me feel good. Somehow, ending a school week with lessons like that used to make me feel on top of the world. I was very timid when I was younger and I would never do anything I was told not to do, but during these lessons I used to come out of myself more. The light-heartedness I felt can only be understood by people who have done the same, one time or another. I enjoyed life in my junior school. I worked hard, because I enjoyed it. I did sports, because I enjoyed it. Everything I did, I wanted to do. However, I must always remember that I was intelligent, I could manage the work easily, I got on well with the teachers because I did as I was told. I make a point of being conscious of this because there are children who are not able to fit into this way of learning . . .

I think I must have written all this because I want to know what I have lost in myself which caused me to feel so discontented and restless. Why, when I was younger could I be content deep inside me, even though there were rules, restrictions and fears? I suppose I accepted everything, whereas now I feel more resentful if anything is forced on me. I cannot feel at peace very often and in a way I am more tense and aggressive. When I say I am more aggressive I do not mean I want to physically fight people, but when people keep bumping into me in the corridor and trivial things like that, I feel more irritated than I should. Sometimes, when I am feeling disgruntled I think, perhaps it is because I find it difficult to accept the fact that I am growing up. If I can tell myself, 'I am never going to be a child again, so I must remember how precious it was, and now I am going to move on,' perhaps I will accept it easier. It is strange that I should find such an inevitable thing hard to accept, but I think I am probably frightened. When I was a child, I could depend on other people whereas now I am more aware of being an individual with my own thoughts. I just want to live my life true to myself and it is not easy.

(May, sixth year)

The final sentence of Sarah's last letter helps to underline how she has decided to take full responsibility from now on, for living her life 'true to myself'. In fact, throughout the many months of her writing these letters, it was very much she who had done the hard thinking and self-searching, gradually helping herself towards clearer thoughts.

3
Thinking it Over

The centre of education is the individual. If we are to achieve a genuinely human education we must return again to the person before us, the child, the adolescent, the adult, the individual who is ready, however dimly and in need of however much support, to adventure both further out into his experience and further into it, who is ready in some part of himself, to risk himself in order to become more than he now is. The teacher, the tutor, can provide conditions and the support for such a journey — but the journey itself can only be made by the assenting and autonomous individual.

Peter Abbs, *Autobiography in Education,* 1974

If Sarah had been seriously ill — too ill to help herself — then it would have been unwise to have tried to help her within the school. Even if we had been skilled enough, no teacher with a normal work-load in a fair-sized comprehensive school could have hoped to offer intensive personal care. On the other hand — assuming that they have the interest and some skills in suggesting directions, and above all the tact that Jim fortunately possessed — then ordinary teachers may be able to offer considerable personal help to people like Sarah without undue demands being made on their time.

The sum of our person-to-person involvement with her was about a dozen visits during 'free' periods and breaks over a year, often when we were at least half-engaged on other things — ordering materials, marking and so on; and a few after-lesson meetings lasting two or three minutes. Many pupils sought out such help, though rarely so consistently as Sarah. Her case led us to realize more clearly that as a department, we were offering — and should continue to offer — an extension to the kind of pastoral care that would have been available from, say, a Head of House who was not actually teaching her at the time. It became a modest but sustained attempt to enact the kind of principle defined by John Macmurray, that 'the capacity to love objectively is the capacity which makes us persons. It is the ultimate source of our capacity to behave in terms of the object. It is the core of rationality.' (*Reason and Emotion,* 1962) The contact offered to Sarah was, in essence, the kind of contact that all teachers might, and do, provide in offering an unaffected interest in their pupils: talking and (especially) listening to them informally, outside the classroom; joining with them in both serious and light-hearted play; and sharing sometimes one's own more private and deeper interests. To know learners in this way will be more valuable than any attempt to know 'about' them, through voluminous studies on 'Psychology in Education', or clinical perusal of school records.

In his posthumously published *The Piggle* (1977) Donald Winnicott describes the progress of a little girl — much younger than Sarah, and more deeply disturbed — during sixteen clinical consultations over a period of two and a half years. Near the end of these sessions, Winnicott recorded that his young patient had made five key achievements: '(1) blooming in age-appropriate maturation; (2) copes with separation and knows that reunion is available; (3) exercising female seductiveness; (4) summing up the analysis, having reorganized her life on a positive transference; (5) thus hate can be safely felt and exercised . . ' Similar improvements could be claimed for Sarah, except perhaps that for the fifth heading it would be more accurate to record for her that 'love (as well as hate) can be safely felt (etc.)'. Winnicott claimed too of his patient that 'I do feel that we must not just think of her in terms of illness. There is much that is healthy in her.' It would have been wrong to think of Sarah in terms of 'illness' — in terms of some condition that separated her from our own experience of pain. Indeed, the progress of loss that she describes, through distress, depression, anger, self-sorrow, towards a gradual return to loving and redemptive feeling, is familiar. It is a difficult, sometimes dangerous journey, rarely survived without injury, and sometimes not survived. My own judgement of the cause of and nature of Sarah's difficulties would be that she was experiencing in an acute form the normal sense of loss of childhood that has to be experienced in adolescence. During this interregnum between childhood and adulthood — a period which is artificially prolonged in our community by the provision of further and higher education, among other influences — the individual must seek for new forms of attachment with people and with the world. No longer can a child's dependence suffice to support the emerging needs of the adult. But irredeemable loss, even necessary loss such as this, sometimes involves an overwhelming *sense* of grief. Reviewing John Bowlby's *Attachment and Loss, Vol 3: Loss, Sadness and Depression* (1980), Denis Harding sums up and comments on Dr Bowlby's description of the normal processes of grief, in a passage which closely corresponds to the patterns of Sarah's letters, and her sense of sorrow as she leaves her childhood:

> Anger, half-refusal to accept the fact, repetitious expressions of grief, compulsive reminiscence, these early responses to a great loss are sometimes difficult for sympathisers to bear with; a reminder, based on psychotherapeutic experience, that we should expect such things is one of the valuable contributions that this book offers.
>
> Denis Harding, 'The process of mourning',
> *The Times Literary Supplement,* July 4th 1980

(This review of Bowlby's book is worth consulting for its analysis of the 'grief' scene in *Macbeth,* when Macduff is told of the murder of his wife and children.) It is in fact the normality of Sarah's experience — normal to herself, normal to ourselves — which deserves attention.

When sections of these letters were shown to fellow teachers, in seminars and meetings, many found them moving. But some teachers admitted a sense of disquiet that Sarah should have set herself so much, and so successfully, against normal school demands. 'Would she have bothered, if you hadn't listened to her in the first place?' 'Isn't she just taking advantage of a soft option, in writing these letters?' 'Is there not a danger in getting ourselves so involved with private lives?' Such doubts have often come from teachers who themselves would claim to respect expressive, personal writing in schools.

Maslow's account in *Towards a Psychology of Being* (1968) of the difficulties of growth is helpful in considering these doubts. Having emphasized that theories of personal growth should be modelled on healthy rather than psychically sick people, he admits that regressive feelings often arise naturally out of normal, healthy growth. Each step forward involves a renouncing of a previously held position, 'even a kind of death prior to rebirth, with consequent nostalgia, fear, loneliness and mourning'. The new life implies greater effort, greater complexity and responsibility. If it is to be met, the individual will need flexibility and courage; and while the learner feels timid, then support will be needed.

Teachers need to respect shyness, to be tactful and unintrusive; but they cannot simply leave shy pupils in their private miseries. Professional helpers can learn how to intervene, support and guide towards further growth; they can help to show that 'dark forces' are as much a part of 'normal' experience as the more familiar 'growth forces'. They also need to acknowledge the learner's capacity fur full self-determination. In practice this will involve acceptance of regressive, as well as progressive states, for the need to look back, to dwell in the still unresolved past, must be accepted as a natural consequence of growing. Maslow suggests a revision of Taoistic 'let-be', to incorporate a principle of active support, of 'helpful let-be', an actively 'loving and respecting Taoism', which recognizes both the fact of growth, and the actual fears and snags, failures and discouragements of growing. In offering to help, we can offer something more than 'merely being hopeful or passively optimistic about it'. There is a duality, even an element of contradiction, in the task of teachers here. They need to reassure shy pupils that their feelings are fully respected, but they can also encourage a search for fresh development. This provides a justification for reading Sarah's letters in the spirit in which they ask to be read; and also, for working *from* them, to offer fresh points of departure for her. It is not enough simply to accept her depressed state (thus conspiring to confirm her morbid views of self and world). Yet neither can her feelings be evaded; in fact the several attempts that we made to side-step the preoccupations of her letters, in trying to lead her back to working 'normally', proved unsuccessful. Through our concern for Sarah we had to learn, in Winnicott's phrase, to 'make positive use of failure' here — to adapt more sensitively to what she needed from us.

Yet it might be argued that if 'normal' work had been insisted on, without exception, from the beginning and across the curriculum, she would not have been able to exploit the 'weak link' of English studies as she had done. It is conceivable that she might have managed to suppress her newly discovered feelings and recollections; and she might have been able to carry on with the patterns of life that she had more or less survived with so far — including extreme shyness, intensive reading in order to escape from the day's realities, and an otherwise unalleviated commitment to her schoolwork. Firmer lines of academic discipline might have led her to renounce the new desires and promptings — the new points of growth — that were coming from within herself. And she might have become a high-achieving academic student. Such arguments were put by some colleagues at the time — sometimes on the crude lines that children, just like dogs, have to be trained and it is our job to do it; sometimes, more plausibly, that there just is not time for sorting out personal problems at Sarah's time of life, when she should be thinking above all about her place on the conveyor belt towards higher education, job prospects and so on. This anxiety about the lack of time available to be patient with meanderings such as those of Sarah in her letters, can be said to reflect the realities of fifth-year learning and teaching, which pushes continually towards what Maslow has termed 'pseudo-growth' — a choking-off of inner promptings, in order to concentrate on making the right kind of impression for external evaluation.

In fact Sarah did not go on to the upper sixth, nor to university. She left at the end of the year to join the local library service. She remained close to Richard, who became a student at a local polytechnic. Her decision against university and against teaching was accepted by her parents, who were disappointed (as we were too). But the signs were that she might have become even more shrinking and unhappy in an academic institution — not, of course, because this is what learning inevitably does to people, but because it would not have been her free decision, in the light of what had newly grown in her, to have gone there. She had needed above all to rescue herself from adopting roles that she had come to feel were not of her choice or making. She saw leaving school and seeking local work as a return to her roots. Her work gave her natural access to the books that she still loved, and she continued to read extensively. She became more confident outwardly, and adopted her own individual professional style, as a librarian. Eventually she married Richard, and when writing to give her consent for the letters to be used for this study she added:

Hearing from you has made me realize how much I have changed, I'm no longer the quiet little person you used to know. I'm still little, but far noisier . . . It may seem old-fashioned but I thoroughly enjoy looking after my two children . . . Soon I will go to evening classes because later on I'm determined to train as a teacher. Having my own children, and also being more confident in myself, I feel more capable of becoming a teacher.

At the moment I've shut myself in the bedroom to quickly write this letter, but Nadine is almost battering the door down so I'll have to go. Unfortunately she has inherited my temper and I daren't risk the consequences!

The writing of school learners can, then, involve no less than the shaping of visions of living that will endure throughout adult life; our task as teachers is to provide the best conditions possible for that shaping to take place.

Notes

1. A more detailed account of the Seriozha-Karenin conflict is provided in my *Learning through Writing* (1983), pp.60-3.

2. For an example of 'paraphrasing' work on *Sons and Lovers* by another member of Sarah's class, please see also op.cit., pp.98-102.

3. The same poem is cited as having provided a means of self-recognition in Sheila MacLeod's account of a young girl's struggle (in her case, via anorexia nervosa) to individuation, in *The Art of Starvation* (1981).

References

Abbs, P. (1974), *Autobiography in Education*. London: Heinemann.

Bowlby, J. (1980), *Attachment and Loss, Vol. 3: Loss, Sadness and Depression*. London: Hogarth Press.

Guntrip, H. (1968), *Schizoid Phenomena: Object Relations and the Self*. London: Tavistock.

Harding, D. (1980), 'The process of mourning' *The Times Literary Supplement*, 4 July, 1980.

Harrison, B.T. (1983), *Learning through Writing*, Windsor: NFER/Nelson.

Hoggart, R. (1958), *The Uses of Literacy*. Harmondsworth: Penguin.

Horney, K. (1950), *Neurosis and Human Growth*. London: Tavistock.

Hourd, M. (1972), *Relationship in Learning*. London: Heinemann.

Lamb, P.F. and Hohlwein, K.J. (1984), *Touchstones: Letters between Two Women, 1953-1965*. London: Julia MacRae.

Lomas, P. (1973), *True and False Experience*. London: Allen Lane.

———— (1981), *The Case for a Personal Psychotherapy*. Oxford University Press.

MacLeod, S. (1981), *The Art of Starvation*. London: Virago.

Maslow, A. (1968), *Towards a Psychology of Being*. New York: Van Nostrand Reinhold.

Macmurray, J. (1962), *Reason and Emotion* (Second Edn). London: Faber.

Smail, D. (1978), *Psychotherapy: A Personal Approach*. London: Dent.

———— (1980), 'Learning in psychotherapy' in *Coming to Know*, Ed. P. Salmon. London: Routledge and Kegan Paul.

Suttie, I. (1935), *The Origins of Love and Hate*. Harmondsworth: Penguin.

Tolstoy, L. (1862) (trans. 1967), 'Education and culture' and 'The school at Yasnaya Polyana' in *Tolstoy on Education* (trans. Weiner 1967). University of Chicago Press.

Winnicott, D. (1965), *The Maturational Processes and the Facilitating Environment*. London: Tavistock.

———— (1971), *Playing and Reality*. London: Tavistock.

———— (1980), *The Piggle*. Harmondsworth: Penguin.